Leave Your Attitude at the Door

Leave Your Attitude at the Door

Dispositions and Field Experiences in Education

Amy Thompson, Crystal Voegele, and Chris Hogan

ROWMAN & LITTLEFIELD
Lanham • Boulder • New York • London

Published by Rowman & Littlefield
A wholly owned subsidiary of The Rowman & Littlefield Publishing Group, Inc.
4501 Forbes Boulevard, Suite 200, Lanham, Maryland 20706
www.rowman.com

Unit A, Whitacre Mews, 26-34 Stannary Street, London SE11 4AB

Copyright © 2017 by Amy Thompson, Crystal Voegele, and Chris Hogan

All rights reserved. No part of this book may be reproduced in any form or by any electronic or mechanical means, including information storage and retrieval systems, without written permission from the publisher, except by a reviewer who may quote passages in a review.

British Library Cataloguing in Publication Information Available

Library of Congress Cataloging-in-Publication Data Available
ISBN 978-1-4758-2708-8 (cloth : alk. paper)
ISBN 978-1-4758-2709-5 (pbk. : alk. paper)
ISBN 978-1-4758-2710-1 (electronic)

∞ ™ The paper used in this publication meets the minimum requirements of American National Standard for Information Sciences Permanence of Paper for Printed Library Materials, ANSI/NISO Z39.48-1992.

Printed in the United States of America

Contents

Acknowledgments		vii
Introduction		xi
1	Pet Peeves about Field Experiences	1
2	Disposition Issues and Aha! Moments	13
3	Different Perspectives and Different Players	23
4	Can You Be Proactive?	37
5	Building Effective Partnerships and Relationships	49
6	Where Do You Go Next?	63
7	Professional Development and Resources	69
Closing Thoughts		75
Master of Arts in Teaching: New Student Orientation		79
Professional Growth Plan		81
Internship Contract		83
Professional Development Plan		85
Professional Agreement		91
About the Authors		93

Acknowledgments

AMY'S ACKNOWLEDGMENTS

First and foremost, I would like to offer unending thanks to my husband, Daniel Thompson, and our son, Matt Thompson, who always support me no matter what dream, goal, or project I have gotten myself into. Their love, encouragement, belief in me, and the way they pick up the slack has not gone unnoticed. It is truly because of them that I could complete this book. My husband's faith in me and my abilities keeps me ever moving forward and on the path to meet my goals.

To my parents, Danny and Karen Earls, thank you for instilling in me a desire to always aim high and shoot for the stars. Your encouragement to fulfill my childhood dreams has led me to where I am today. My mom always said I would write a book one day and kept encouraging me to finish by reminding me that I have wanted to do this since falling in love with books as a child.

To my sister, Melissa Earls, I know the readers thank you for your amazing editorial work, and I thank you for always being there when I need you. Your creative eye resulted in a beautiful cover.

To Deborah Mitchell, my first principal, you always encouraged me and saw great things in my future—far before I could even imagine them. Thank you for taking a chance on that first-year, no-experience teacher and letting me live my dream and run with whatever wild and crazy method, strategy, or idea I could cook up next.

To my students, from my first fourth-grade class to my current graduate students, thank you for allowing me into your lives, teaching me more than I could ever imagine, and reminding me that I continue to live my true calling every day.

To Dr. Tammy Benson, thank you for taking a chance on me and giving me my first university opportunity. Your servant leadership and guidance continue to offer me opportunities I could have only dreamed of. It is an honor to call you friend.

Finally, to my co-authors Crystal Voegele and Chris Hogan, we make an amazing team, and all the laughs, tears, and inappropriate words made every moment of this journey worthwhile.

CRYSTAL'S ACKNOWLEDGMENTS

I would like to say a special thank you to my husband, Tom Voegele, who has always supported my big dreams, loving and nurturing my spirit to learn and grow.

To my children, thank you for allowing me to be a mom and a writer, inspiring me incessantly.

To my parents, Bo and Janet Blankenship, you gave me the confidence to persevere through adversity and trials, thank you.

To my teachers who helped me discover my voice, thank you. Dr. Jamie Alea, thank you for showing me the path to and through the fields we weave and work. To my students, all of you, thank you for teaching me the value of teaching and reaffirming my call.

To my co-writers, it has been a pleasure learning from two pioneers in education. Amy Thompson is, undoubtedly, one of the hardest working women I know and is also one of the most passionate educators in existence. Her love for teaching is only matched by her love for children. Chris Hogan served the schools in many capacities; her knowledge and wit flow from an abundant spring of wisdom and kindness. Her generous heart, impeccable insight, and unbeatable work ethic are just a few traits that distinguish her in our field. It has truly been an honor to work with two such wonderful educators.

CHRIS' ACKNOWLEDGMENTS

I would like to thank my husband, Rusty Hogan, for his support during this process. He encourages me by asking "Why not?" instead of "Why?" as I continue to progress in my career and explore my future. His honesty and care for me, my parents, and my daughter help me to understand the value of the phrase, "I've got your back."

Thanks also to my daughter, Samantha, who inspires me and continuously pushes me to improve through her commitment and creativity in her life as a physical therapist and wife. I love and admire her more than I can ever express. She is my touchstone, my most honest critic, and my support when I need it the most.

I would like to acknowledge my parents, George and Beth Schichtl. Dad taught me that we are only limited by our lack of imagination and our commitment to a task, and Mom taught me never to forget the power of a caring attitude. I also want to thank my brothers for helping me to learn that you can accomplish more together than you can alone.

To my principals and administrators, Robert Toney, Steve Fulmer, Ray Simon, and Philip Bell, thank you for being great role models who exemplified the benefits of having a good sense of humor, the quality of instruction that a good instructional leader creates, the empowerment that a leader provides with honest answers and a caring attitude, and the limitless possibilities you provide for teachers and students when they come to you with ideas and you tell them to "show me your ideas and explain how you plan to accomplish them." They inspired and empowered me during my career.

Finally, I would like to thank my department chair, Tammy Benson, for her support. She not only welcomes our feedback and ideas, she promotes it. I could not have written a word of this book without my co-authors, Amy Thompson and Crystal Voegele. They are creative, committed, and hilarious. They are an inspiration both personally and professionally. I am blessed to have them for colleagues and for friends.

Introduction

REALITY CHECK: IDEAS AND EXPERIENCES MEET ACTUAL IMPLEMENTATION

When asked to write this book, we were truly honored, yet confused. Who are we to tell anyone how to do anything? As much as we sometimes would like to think we know it all, we know that ultimately, we will never be the holders of all knowledge. We're not doctors—yet. We are clinical instructors, teachers straight from the classroom living their dreams in higher education, determined to make education better for all. While we were at the top of the class in the classroom, here we are now coordinating field experience, while at times feeling like first-year teachers all over again.

I would like to tell you that we immediately walked into our jobs, read the manual, and set the world on fire for education. Unfortunately, there was no manual. But there were fires. And we had to extinguish them—quickly and with finesse.

Everything we know we have learned from experience. It is a lot of trial and error and constant tweaking. We are continually responsive to our students', school partners', and university's needs. It's a must. Picture if you will a juggler, and you will get an idea of a day in the life of a field coordinator.

When asked to write this book, we thought—a research book on field? Citations? APA? MLA? Footnotes? What? However, we quickly learned that we were called to write this book from our experiences—what we do, what we've tried, what works. *That* we know. Education is ever changing, and we refuse to become stagnant.

So, when asked if we were interested in writing a book on teacher preparation field experience, we answered with a resounding "Yes." We love field. We love it because it changes, it's never boring, it's a giant puzzle with constantly changing rules, and it keeps us in the schools.

Field experience is the capstone. It's what makes teachers teachers. It's where the action is. For us, it keeps us current and relevant, and that is what makes us good at our jobs.

COMMON VOCABULARY

Throughout the book you will see several terms used interchangeably. Candidates, interns, and students are all referring to the students in our program who are in the field in some capacity. Interns, student teachers, and preservice teachers refer to those candidates out in the field in their final, capstone, internship semester. Our mentor teachers are the teachers with which we place our students while in internship; they are also referred to as cooperating teachers. In the context of our book, teacher education refers to preservice teachers. All programs that we refer to are initial licensure programs. Finally, supervisors who go out and observe, assist, and grade the interns during their internship experience are also referred to as university supervisors or even faculty.

WHY "LEAVE YOUR ATTITUDE AT THE DOOR"?

When approached about this book, we were doing a presentation at the Association of Teacher Educators conference on dispositional issues in the field. We shared stories of big attitudes that are large and in charge and which have to be nipped in the bud. This does not have to be someone "in your face." It can be someone lazy, without a work ethic, or even someone chronically tardy. Attitude is how our candidates reflect or impose themselves in the classroom. The door? That is the field.

At the university level, professors generally take care of their own classroom issues. However, we have all seen those students who are great on paper. You know, the 4.0 student. But when you put them in a classroom, what happens? They go down faster than the Titanic—becoming someone you do not even recognize.

Dispositional issues have become a major college- and university-wide issue. School districts can shut us down because of one issue. It has happened. The quality of our interns has an immediate, profound, long-lasting impact on our partnerships with relationships with schools. Therefore, we have to have a system in place to deal with any and all issues as they arise. This book is about our system.

WHO ARE WE?

You must be asking—*who are these people?* What experience do they have? What gives them the street cred to be able write this book about their system?

Amy Thompson

As of the writing of this book, I am entering my fourth year as a clinical instructor, field placement coordinator, and program coordinator for the Master of Arts in Teaching (MAT) program in the Department of Teaching and Learning at the University of Central Arkansas.

My field includes placements for practicum and internship candidates. There are several hats to my field coordinator job: I work, alongside with Crystal and her undergraduates, to train our placed MAT candidates as they fulfill their internship requirements. When issues arise, I work closely with candidates, teachers, administrators, and the university to ensure all parties are heard, to reach mutually beneficial outcomes, and to create professional improvement plans and contracts with candidates to ensure improvement is made and situations are resolved.

Not only do I work with interns, I also create and conduct supervisor trainings and work collaboratively with supervisors and mentor teachers to ensure internship runs like a well-oiled machine. Since our program is an online program, I create virtual Screencasts of these trainings for our mentor teachers and candidates living a great distance from campus.

As the MAT program coordinator, I work closely with the graduate school to admit new students, lead the team in curriculum revisions and program improvements, and tirelessly work with our candidates as they apply for and interview for jobs where I can then guide them through the provisional licensure process. My door is always open, and you will generally find students coming in and out seeking advice and counsel. While I have chairs in there, I jokingly say I'm going to replace those chairs with a couch and hang a sign that says, "The Doctor is IN."

As a clinical instructor, I live the dream. Teaching teachers is what I always wanted to do, and not only do I get to teach teachers, but I get to teach them something I'm passionate about—reading assessments, difficulties, and interventions. As part of this course, I supervise my students as they work in our college's BearsRead Reading Camp, and it gives me an opportunity to continue to give back and make a difference. I still get to work with kids in a really fun environment.

I am also a National Board Certified Teacher in literacy. I coordinate our university's support site each year, assisting area teachers in obtaining scholarships for the process and guiding them through the process to become certified. Having recently renewed my certification, our site decided to open the doors to renewal candidates as well, and we have a great time on Saturday mornings becoming more reflective teachers and improving our practice across the state.

Prior to working in higher education, I worked in the Little Rock School District teaching third and fourth grades for fourteen years. During my tenure, I thrived in leadership opportunities. I served as grade-level chair, chaired the technology committee, served as the teacher representative on the parent teacher association, and chaired numerous district committees.

I led professional development for the district in math and science, and I was Pathwise and Teacher Excellence Support System (TESS) trained, giving me the ability to serve as a mentor teacher to student teachers and novice teachers to the profession. One of my biggest accomplishments is that I designed and implemented a web page for every individual teacher in our building, and we hosted our own site—a first for our district. I was the first National Board Certified Teacher in my building, and I won the Volunteer in Public Schools Teacher of the Year Award. Numerous times, my colleagues nominated me as our school's teacher of the year, and I proudly represented my school at the district level.

Personally, I am married, and we have one adult son and five dogs. I love to read, watch movies, travel, and spend time with my family.

In my spare time, I am also a doctoral candidate at the University of Central Arkansas, pursuing a PhD in interdisciplinary leadership.

Crystal Voegele

At this moment in time, I am a clinical instructor and field placement coordinator for middle-level and secondary programs in the Department of Teaching and Learning at the University of Central Arkansas; I have served in this capacity for three years. My field includes placements for early field, Internship I, and Internship II candidates. As part of my coordinator job, not only do I place our candidates, but I (along with an array of experts in the field) train our candidates as they maneuver and learn the ways of school life. When issues arise, as they sometimes do, I am also the liaison between the university and the schools.

I also provide supervisor trainings and work collaboratively with supervisors and mentors to design trainings for our candidates. In addition to working with mentors, supervisors, and candidates, I am also frequently in transit, seeking new, innovative alliances and partnerships. Along with working as a clinical instructor and coordinator of field placement, I am also a doctoral candidate at the University of Memphis, seeking a degree in higher education administration.

Prior to my induction as instructor at the University of Central Arkansas, I served as a classroom teacher, serving for fourteen years as a middle-level literacy teacher. Allow me to say that I love teaching, and middle school teaching is where it is at! One of my fields you will read about highlights a field-based course I teach that is housed at a middle school, working with actual middle-level students. I may be a tad partial.

During my tenure as a classroom teacher, I worked in Little Rock School District, Greenbrier School District, and Conway Public Schools. As a classroom teacher, I served in many leadership capacities and also mentored several teacher candidates. From Pathwise to Teacher Excellence Support System (TESS), Charlotte Danielson's Teacher Excellence Model, I lived through the myriad evaluations teachers are facing today. I served on curriculum committees, technology committees, and professional development committees, finding teacher leadership as rewarding as teaching itself and realizing throughout my time as a teacher the true value and necessity for quality teacher education and professional development—preservice and ongoing.

As a child, I was called to teach and that call continues today. Leading future teachers, serving as a guidepost for them as they sojourn through this exciting career, is a passion that I have the opportunity to explore daily.

Chris Hogan

Currently, I am a clinical instructor at the University of Central Arkansas. I have been an educator for forty years. My first teaching experience was in Title I in a suburban school's district. Then I taught fifth grade for twelve years.

I moved to middle school and taught sixth-grade social studies for four years before applying to a smaller district as elementary principal. After I got over the shock of the difference in facilities and supplies in a smaller, rural district, I found my feet and learned to be a good scavenger and creative budgeter. Our elementary school grew, improved, and formed partnerships with our co-op and the University of Central Arkansas.

Fifteen years after I arrived at the elementary school, I left a much better facility with outstanding teachers and staff to move to a position at the central office in the district. This position gave me an opportunity to learn about and report on our federal programs, mentor and new teacher programs, and our district's Arkansas Comprehensive School Improvement Planning Plan (ACSIP).

I retired from public schools in 2006 and was invited to teach a class with the MAT program at the university. I had forgotten how much I enjoyed teaching. Each semester, I learn as much from my students as they learn from me. My experience as a lead teacher, elementary principal, and administrator for federal and state programs has really helped me with the field experience courses I teach.

I love helping students find their way as they begin teaching. I enjoy helping them to learn to use their personalities to become more effective teachers that can enjoy their careers. Helping interns find connections with their students that open the doors for learning, exploring, and conversing is one of the greatest feelings you can have.

JOIN US ON OUR JOURNEY

You will quickly discover that we believe laughter is the best medicine, and we love to tell stories. We would rather laugh than cry, and we do! We laugh *a lot*, and we hope you laugh with us too. It is our hope that not only do you enjoy the book but that some of our trial by fire experiences can help you as you encourage your candidates to "Leave Your Attitude at the Door."

ONE
Pet Peeves about Field Experiences

First, let us address a disclaimer—this chapter could be its own book. Addressing pet peeves in our profession is not exactly what we set out to do when surmising to author a book concerning intern dispositions; however, this is fundamental in establishing the very need and purpose of such a book. Managing intern dispositions is only a small piece to the enormity of what we really do; however, our handling of such issues and attitudes comprises a larger, more significant place in the totality of field placement coordination and the establishment of viable partnerships.

Who would expect to meet unprofessional people and unprofessional behavior in the most honorable of professions—education? But we have all been there. Not a week goes by where we do not encounter or hear stories of teachers making bad decisions that ultimately impact students.

Sad is the day when interns are removed from internship programs due to poor decision making and dispositional issues. Are teacher preparatory programs to blame when they do not have responsive programming and interventions in place to redirect interns in need? How do teacher preparatory programs ensure they are not part of the problem?

Ensuring fairness, consistency, and equitability are vital when experiences meet implementation. We know we have problems; therefore, we must design solutions that work because the reality is that we will continue to encounter dispositional issues from interns. What must change are our attitudes and our approaches. We have to change to experience a change.

> OUR TOP TEN PET PEEVES ABOUT FIELD EXPERIENCE
>
> 1. The Placement Process in a World of Stalkers and Talkers
> 2. The Rules Don't Apply to Me
> 3. Rude, Crude, and Socially Unacceptable
> 4. This Ain't Your Momma's Kitchen
> 5. Woe is Me: Working with Mentors
> 6. Communication 101
> 7. Code of Unethics
> 8. You Mean I Have to Get up Before 8:00 a.m.?
> 9. Those with Attitudes Need Not Apply
> 10. What We Have Here is a Failure to Take Responsibility

THE PLACEMENT PROCESS IN A WORLD OF STALKERS AND TALKERS

The placement process in and of itself is a tremendous undertaking, and every aspect of it can quickly become a pet peeve. From the initial paperwork a student fills out requesting placement to the student walking through the school door, a million things can and do go awry.

You think it would be easy. A student fills out paperwork requesting placement. You process the paperwork, ensuring grade point, courses, and background checks are in order. Contact is made to school administrators requesting a placement. Administrators assign a teacher, and you convey that to the student. Voila! Placement success!

If only it were that easy.

Paperwork is tedious. Placement packets are submitted incomplete, and requests are sometimes made long past the deadline. Who knew we would have to deal with so much paper before people?

Contacts with schools are constantly changing, and the players are different in each location. You may work with the principal, assistant principal, instructional coach, human resources officer, or even the librarian. Once you figure out with whom you're working, the stalking begins.

In this cat-and-mouse game, the chase begins when an email is sent requesting placement in a school. Even though we thought this streamlined process would ensure our capture of the coveted placement, it may still be just beyond our reach. The snag? The email request goes unanswered. Trying to lure our prey without scaring them off, we resend those email requests. Many times. Why, you ask? Every administrator or contact does not use email, may only check it once a week, or prioritizes their email responses—universities are not generally the priority.

At this point, we have to rev up our stalking and take the chase to the phones. Sometimes these phone requests escalate to daily phone calls. Anything we have to do to get that placement. While we haven't had to go make an in-person placement request yet, it is not out of the question.

The stalking doesn't just end there. Once the student is notified of their field placement, *their* stalking begins. Students will frequent school websites and Facebook and will talk to anyone who might know their assigned teacher to find out the dirt. They will research and latch onto any bit of information—verified or not.

One student used his stalking skills and learned his teacher was a coach and did not teach in a regular classroom situation. They dug further through the gossip mill and heard this was not a desirable or effective teacher. When brought to our attention, we then have to follow up on these rumors. Of course, we discovered the teacher was teaching math and was highly recommended by the administration.

So it's important to verify information gathered from research before acting on it. We could have pulled a placement from a wonderful mentor had we not investigated the results of a student's "stalking." As you can see, stalking is definitely a part of the job description—not just our own stalking but students, too. We truly have become masters at the game.

THE RULES DON'T APPLY TO ME

Whenever you work with a variety of people, you run across individuals who feel the "rules don't apply to me." Each semester, we encounter students who embrace this motto. These students create problems not only for us in field placement, but they also create problems for themselves.

Experience in this arena has taught us at the university level that we are upon the Age of Entitlement. Heralding in this new age is an emerging group of future educators who believe themselves to hold the key to the mysteries of education. They know more than university seminars offer. They often approach us with scheduling conflicts regarding our meeting dates for orientation or seminars and are quick to include that they know the information that will be covered already.

As we try to work with them and delve deeper into the problem, we often learn they do not want to make the drive or feel they know what they need to do and the meeting is just a waste of time. The following are examples of a few comments written by interns on their exit slips:

- "I could present this material myself."
- "When it comes to professionalism and interviewing, I know all there is to know. This is redundant information."

Sadly, many of our "entitled interns" are still unemployed—even though they claim know more than their seasoned mentors. Every semester, we know which interns will complain about their mentors' lack of knowledge and professionalism. "My mentor can't teach," said an intern recently when pulled in for a conference regarding her own professionalism. Incredibly, the mentor in question's students' scores on formal assessments are the top in the state, and both students and parents regard her as excellent. She received the coveted Teacher of the Year title this very year.

Without fail, we have students who miss mandatory meetings because they simply forgot. They don't even bother concocting an excuse. Paperwork requirements and state-mandated trainings are sometimes disregarded. Only the threat of not being allowed to enter internship gets these tasks completed. Too often, students are above the deadlines and requirements.

Another indicator of their feelings of entitlement include being too "busy" to get involved at their school sites. Mentors will normally let it slip when an intern is beating the buses out of the parking lot after school or when they drag in after the bell rings in the morning. We also get calls when mentors are attending meetings, sponsoring events, or attending parent-teacher conferences and the intern is MIA.

The end results of the Age of Entitlement for the entitled intern is a semester filled with miscommunication, incorrect assignments, and problems with their mentors and the field experience office. "Disregarding the rules is okay when you are entitled and above them," said no teacher.

RUDE, CRUDE, AND SOCIALLY UNACCEPTABLE

On occasion, we encounter students who do not fit the teacher persona. Let's be real for a moment. Many of us have had teachers who we all wondered how and why they joined the education profession. Just reading the title of this section might have brought a certain unprofessional teacher to your mind. Oh, the stories we could all tell about unprofessional teachers with whom we have had first-hand experiences.

We know all interns have to start somewhere, and we are their first stop on their journey as teachers. All too often, we hear about these prospective teachers long before they grace our internship programs. Many develop reputations in college and, subsequently, in early field as being troublemakers.

We have seen it all when it comes to these developing new teachers:

- The cussing teachers
- The boozing teachers
- The smelly teachers
- The dressed inappropriately teachers

- The teacher who tells their mentors off
- The teacher who tells their students off
- The teacher who tells the students and their mentors too much
- The lying teachers
- And many, many more

Most of our students who struggle in early field and education coursework come from one or more of these categories of unprofessionalism.

As a matter of fact, one student managed to pass all of his tests and all of his courses, but he consistently struggled with field, due—according to him—to his mentors. Every mentor he had been placed with was "out to get him." Interviews with mentors were conducted, and the findings were disturbing. He had developed a habit of helping himself to a mentor's desk, computer, files, and personal snacks; in addition, he also would blurt out answers to the teacher's questions meant for students and correct (often *incorrectly*) all of his mentors during their lessons.

Forging attendance sheets, failing to meet with his mentor, and showing up late were more problems the candidate faced. He never took responsibility for his constant display of unprofessionalism. He complained to anyone who would listen and also divulged many personal details about his life to his mentors and his students. But on paper, this guy looked great! His professors raved of his knowledge, but when it came to the actual classroom and practical application of his knowledge, he struggled immensely. The school he was placed with actually banned him!

When these rogue future teachers arrive, again, their reputations often precede them, and, more often than not, we are ready; having a plan in place is vital. Developing strong partnerships, mentor teachers, supervising teachers, and intervention plans are a must for any successful program.

THIS AIN'T YOUR MOMMA'S KITCHEN

We often joke that being a field placement coordinator is equivalent to being a firefighter, and in so many ways, this is true. From preventing fires to putting fires out, we are always on call to handle whatever emergencies arise, and all too often, in spite of the best planning and preparation, someone still gets burned.

Who hasn't had a mentor upset with the lack of preparation of an intern? What about a mentor upset with the university over their mishandling of an intern issue or training? Have you ever had interns who failed to follow protocol? What about when a supervisor decides to give an administrator a piece of her mind?

I'm sure none of you have encountered an intern who overstepped his boundaries and destroyed a mentor's desire to ever mentor again. What about when a situation gets so destructive a school no longer wants to partner? Who can forget the mentor who inspires an intern right out of the profession? Smelly interns, inappropriate interns, know-it-all interns, bossy mentors, passive mentors, super supervisors, lazy supervisors; we have seen it all.

Cleaning up after others is a pet peeve that is considered a workplace hazard in the field placement arena, and much like facing a real fire, we have learned—often the hard way—some valuable tips that will help any and all who work in this rewarding field. We will go to great lengths discussing ways to be proactive in this profession; in addition, we will also prepare you for the unexpected fire that will inevitably cross your path.

WOE IS ME: WORKING WITH MENTORS

Working in education entitles one to be an expert in woes, especially when working with mentors. Most mentors know teaching and desire to share their love and passion for the profession by nurturing and growing future teachers. We value our mentors and the sacrifice they each make when committing to the enormous task of training a teacher with little to no experience. It is a big job.

Being fresh from the classroom, we know the challenges that mentors are currently facing. From new teacher evaluation systems to evolving curriculums and ever-changing student assessments and accountability, mentors are wearing many hats and balancing many duties. Quality mentors are precious gems meant to be valued and respected by the universities they serve.

Mentor selection is no easy task, and as many field placement coordinators and directors will attest, it is a never-ending, always changing, and extremely challenging balancing act. We match mentors and interns, interns and supervisors, and mentors and supervisors, which results in field placement coordinators being the cupids of the colleges of education. One issue with one relationship can create, once again, a firestorm where relationships are ultimately severed and partnerships possibly destroyed.

In reality, not all mentors should mentor, and, sadly, this is often not discovered until it is too late. We have encountered mentors who violate confidences and attempt to destroy the reputations of interns and the college. Occasionally, we see mentors who struggle with their own classroom management and, in essence, feed their interns to the wolves. There are cases we have dealt with involving mentor unprofessionalism where interns ultimately pay the price. Recruiting and retaining high-quality mentors is only one piece of the placement puzzle.

Great mentors can struggle with certain interns. It is the duty of the university to form strong partnerships and communication to ensure optimal matching when it comes to the intern, the mentor, and supervisor. Personality conflicts can and do happen, but having a plan in place for when issues arise and being proactive in training both mentors and supervisors are vital.

COMMUNICATION 101

Communication issues are prolific throughout the field experience process. There are so many players that a breakdown in communication, somewhere, is inevitable. Field experience personnel try to convey that we can't fix it if we don't know about it. To help with communication, we try to set forth a very clear communication structure or chain of command: mentor teachers to university supervisors to field coordinators to program directors to department chair to dean.

What we discover is that when mentors and interns do not communicate, we have an immediate breakdown. Interns do not always ask for feedback, and mentors do not always offer feedback. Some mentor–intern pairs can suffer in silence an entire semester when, had we known about the issues, we could have acted upon them resulting in a positive experience for the mentor and significant improvement for the intern.

Other times, mentors have problems with their interns, do not communicate this to their intern, and jump right to the field coordinator or program director—completely bypassing the university supervisor. The same has been true of interns. In this instance, something that can be an easy-to-solve problem has escalated to a four-alarm fire! If communication does not happen between mentors and interns, we have a mess to clean up or a fire to put out. Our first line of attack is to ensure they are communicating. If only mentors and interns were open and honest from the beginning, we could give up our firefighter hats!

As field coordinators, we have an open door policy and are available by call, text, email, or face-to-face. Even with all of that help and support in place, issues still occur. Our top communication woes include:

- Mentor teachers and supervisors not making us aware of issues
- Mentor teachers and interns taking school business to social media
- Interns not respecting confidentiality

In some instances, we have discovered that interns or mentors are communicating with everyone but us. We have discovered problems from other teachers in the school or even other interns. What does this do? It spreads that fire even more. Remember the old adage, "Loose lips sink ships?" That is definitely true in the field of education.

The ultimate communication problem results in a tremendous loss to the profession. When mentors do not communicate problems they're having, they suffer in silence. After this suffering, they refuse to mentor with us again. In many cases, we have lost an excellent mentor, and many times those are in short supply!

A loss of any mentor is a detriment. The same happens with interns. When interns do not communicate problems they're having and suffer in silence, they have no one to come in and mediate to help resolve the problem. Instead, we have had interns just drop internship and/or the program without ever hearing of an issue. That is a loss to our college as we have a student make it that far only to quit—without our support. Both of these instances we like to avoid at all costs!

CODE OF UNETHICS

To say some interns struggle with adjusting to the professional workplace is a gross understatement. Some struggle to the point teaching becomes no longer a possibility. Many of the issues we see most frequently stem from a clear lack of common sense. Inappropriate talk with students, teachers, and parents is often encountered. Misappropriate use of social media, violating confidentiality, and even using tobacco and drugs while supervising students have been entertained by our field office.

We have all had those situations where we walk away going, "Who in their right mind would have done that?" We have seen blatant, obvious violations of the ethical standards set forth by our state, and despite intensive, explicit trainings, violations continue and dreams of teaching die in their wake.

We strive to prevent unethical behaviors because prevention is the key here. Once behaviors and violations are evident, it is extremely difficult to regain confidences and the respect of our partners and mentors. Occasionally, depending on the severity of the offense, we have provided interventions; however, we seek to be proactive first.

In addition to outlining our proactive measures, we will also delve into establishing contracts and interventions along with how we handle the removal of interns from the teacher education program. Establishing open communication and building trusting relationships with our mentors and partner schools are a must when the sad occasion arises where an intern's ethics are in question.

YOU MEAN I HAVE TO GET UP BEFORE 8:00 A.M.?

Picture this: It's a cool September day. A school bell rings at 8:00 a.m., signaling the beginning of the day. The principal comes over the intercom to give the morning announcements. A class of twenty-eight fifth graders is all in attendance. Sounds like a normal school day, right?

There is a little problem. No teacher! And this isn't the first time this has happened. This is the third time this week, and it's only Wednesday. What do you think is going to happen? If you were that fifth grader, what sort of mischief could you get into with no teacher supervising you, and you were in a room with twenty-seven other children? This could be a picture of an intern's class. For some, attendance is a real problem.

Attendance problems include tardies, absences, and failure to report absences. In a mid-semester disposition survey, one mentor teacher marked a student's attendance as "acceptable" and then commented, "She gets to school tardy a little more often than she should." Digging a little deeper, we discovered this intern was tardy two or three days a week on average. Not acceptable. But, mentor teachers don't always readily let us know of this issue.

Teachers are nurturers. They're problem solvers. They take responsibility for everything that happens in their classroom—whether it's in their control or not. Teachers take it personally when someone under their watch doesn't do what they're supposed to, and some think a misstep by an intern is a reflection on them. We diligently work to convey just the opposite. As mentors, you can do everything right and model every appropriate behavior, and interns will still be absent or tardy.

In some of our programs, students are required to report to school the first day teachers are back on contract at the beginning of the semester—not the first day the students return or the first day the university is back. Our students are told this is part of their field experience and absences must be made up. Our students are instructed on how to easily communicate with both our office and the school when they will be absent.

It's October, and the semester is going well. We are nearing midterms, and a casual conversation starts about an intern. We discover our student reported to her mentor teacher that she would have to miss the first week of school due to illness. Having no record of that, we checked in with the university supervisor. The student reported to the supervisor that our office had approved her absence due to scheduling issues with her children since school had not started yet. The truth? A Hawaiian vacation.

THOSE WITH ATTITUDES NEED NOT APPLY

Working with hundreds of students a semester from undergraduate early field to undergraduate internship to graduate-level internship, it is a given we will encounter multiple types of personalities, sometimes in one student. Yes, that has happened. If you think that all aspiring teachers are calm, even-tempered, happy, eager people, let us dispel that myth. They're not.

If you think all aspiring teachers are eager, respectful, anxious learners, let us dispel that one, too. They're not. And, if you think that all aspiring teachers have a positive attitude, let us really dispel that myth. They're not. Personalities are abundant, and attitudes are not left at the door.

Our students are coming out more prepared than ever before. But, any teacher will tell you that earning that 4.0 in coursework doesn't mean you're knowledgeable enough to be a rock star in the field. And just because something works in a university classroom doesn't mean it will work in the clinical setting. Therefore, field experience is crucial in teacher preparation.

Our students need to put into practice what they have learned and see an expert model best practices. Not every student understands they are *still learning while in the field*. We have encountered a few know-it-alls. You know the type. You can't tell them anything. They're always right, and they are not afraid to tell you how a lesson really should have been taught or how a situation really should have been handled. For some, we may need a refresher in, "If you can't say anything nice, don't say anything at all."

WHAT WE HAVE HERE IS A FAILURE TO TAKE RESPONSIBILITY

When problems surface during field experiences, it is refreshing when the intern and/or the mentor teacher accept responsibility for them. However, there are those moments where personal responsibility goes out the window. This begins with orientation for field experiences.

Invariably, there are students who do not want to wait for the required meetings. Students will be so eager that they attempt to go out and make their own placements—in schools that only work with placement officers or that only accept undergraduates and not graduates (or vice versa). This results in the dreaded "clean-up on Aisle Field."

Even after a directive is given to not contact a school under any circumstances, students will try to work around the system and then not accept the responsibility when it inevitably goes awry. For the student, it is everyone else's fault. In early field, they are new at this and nobody told them what to do. Did we mention that we have handbooks, web pages, text messages, emails, and informational meetings? In practicum, they beg for an exception to the meetings, assignments, and placement rules. In internship, it is always the mentor teacher's fault. Or the supervisor's fault. Or Chalk and Wire's fault. Or Blackboard's fault. Or the field coordinator's fault. The list goes on.

The students are not the only ones with responsibility issues. For the mentor, the student cannot or will not follow directions. The student has it out for them. The student needs more experience. Wait a minute? Aren't they there to get experience? Sometimes, mentor teachers need to remember—they were once interns, too. Everyone has to start somewhere.

Invariably, these problems tend to end up in the lap of the field placement coordinator— often bypassing even the supervising college instructor. Mentors want the issues resolved but often do not feel comfortable addressing the student directly about it. Interns do not want to take the responsibility of initiating a sit-down discussion with the intern and would rather we solve their communication problem. It is time to don our fire gear again. There are fires to put out—all in the name of a lack of personal responsibility.

THE SILVER LINING

Do any of these examples resonate with you? Did you find yourself nodding in agreement as you read through the list? Did you experience a little shock and awe? Rest assured, there is a silver lining!

While we share some of our most extreme examples with you, we will also walk you through how to manage those tumultuous times. In every story, there is a silver lining. We have learned something. We have used that issue to further develop our program, and we have taken this knowledge and become proactive, not reactive, through the process.

While this job is not for the faint of heart, it is for people who are passionate—passionate about kids, passionate about teachers, passionate about education. We would be remiss if we didn't let you know that we absolutely love our jobs, helping to shape and mold future educators as well as keeping our thumb on the pulse of education by staying in close contact with teachers and administrators while keeping a presence in the schools.

Not only are we present in schools, but we are making a difference in those schools through our creation of innovative field experience opportunities and programs. While it is easy to get caught up in the woes of field experience, there are many things to be celebrated.

Whether you are a classroom teacher seeking guidance as mentor teacher, a university supervisor needing assistance, or a field placement coordinator wishing to enhance your practice and outreach, we offer simple yet proven approaches to working with interns, supervisors, mentors, and partnerships to ensure, ultimately, the very best, knowledgeable, and professional teachers enter the profession.

TWO
Disposition Issues and Aha! Moments

Sometimes, unbelievably, kindergarten concepts appear to be very difficult for some college students. It never ceases to amaze us that some of the basic concepts of behavior at school do not seem to transfer from the high school classroom to college field experiences. Attendance, tardiness, professional dress, cell phone etiquette, social media, and professionalism are all issues we have learned to address during orientation. Even then, we receive communications from public schools and mentors complaining about student candidates who do not follow the guidelines we set up.

What happens? Where do some students get such a feeling of entitlement? What happened to common sense? How in the world can we handle these issues proactively? Some of the dispositions issues we address include the following.

1. ATTENDANCE/TARDINESS—SHOW UP

So, the semester has begun. Students have attended an orientation where requirements, etiquette, professionalism, and everything about field experience we can think of have been explained. All questions have been answered, and everyone is on the same page . . . or are we?

Each semester we have students who must wait for placements. Due to the number of students we place and the need to find schools that are in relatively close proximity to the candidate's residence, it can occasionally take us two to four weeks to find classrooms and teachers for placements. We cover this in orientation and caution teacher candidates not to panic.

Some candidates contact us constantly to see if we have found a placement for them. Some are content to wait until they hear from us. Once placements have been confirmed, candidates are notified and asked to contact the school to schedule their observation times. That is where the next set of problems begins. Some teacher candidates rush into the schools and give their mentor teacher a list of times that will be convenient for them to observe. This is in spite of our instructions during orientation to listen to the teacher explain his or her schedule and ask about the best times to observe. This is not a great first impression for establishing a partnership with the teacher.

Other teacher candidates only email the school—other modes of communication not occurring to them. After a week or more with no response, they call us to see what they need to do. When we ask them if they have been to the school to introduce themselves or picked up the phone and called the school, they sound surprised. "Do I need to go by or call? I sent them an email." Meanwhile, the teacher who agreed to help the student is wondering where the student is and if he or she even knows a teacher mentor has been assigned.

Each district has a protocol that must be followed. Larger districts require we contact the central office and their personnel contact the schools and administrators. In smaller districts, we contact the principals directly, and they tell us if teachers are available to mentor our candidates. In spite of checking, double-checking, and following up, we have situations each semester where our teacher candidates go to the school office to be escorted to a classroom where the teacher is informed for the first time that they will have an observer from the university.

Getting the student into the classroom does not solve the problem of showing up. Somehow, somewhere between graduation for high school and field experience, the art of punctuality is lost. If the candidate is scheduled to be in the classroom at 8:00 then, apparently for some candidates, 8:15, 8:30, or even 9:00 is close enough. Then they wonder why the teacher is in a "bad mood."

Naturally, there are times when the teacher candidate does not feel well. Surprisingly, many do not see the importance of contacting their supervising teacher. It never occurs to them that the teacher might have planned a lesson that relied on their assistance, or it could even be the teacher candidate's day to teach a lesson he or she has planned.

Occasionally, candidates experience a death in their families and must miss for several days. Normally, if mentor teachers are contacted, they are understanding and helpful. Unfortunately, it has been our experience that, for some candidates, these untimely deaths seem to coincide with the dates of a cruise or vacation. When they post photos on Facebook or other social media and have "friended" their mentor teacher and others in the school, they are surprised to find out there are questions about truthfulness when they return to observe.

We have learned that requiring students to submit contact information for their supervising teacher as soon as they meet them for the first time can help with a lot of these issues. When we receive the information, we send the supervising teachers an email thanking them for their help and giving them our contact information in case they have problems. We also contact them throughout the semester with information and requests to let us know if they need any help.

ENTERING CONTACT INFORMATION AND TAKING RESPONSIBILITY

- Enter your name.
- Enter the name of your mentor teacher or the name of the teacher who is supervising you during your practicum experience in the school.
- Enter the email address of your mentor/supervising teacher. Type this information *exactly* as you would type it in an email message.
- Verify the email address you entered by entering it again. Are you sure that it is accurate?
- Who is responsible for checking to see that email communication between your instructor and your mentor/supervising teacher has been successful?

---

2. BE PREPARED AND PROFESSIONAL

Being prepared is not just for scouts. We expect our students to come to school dressed appropriately and prepared to help their supervising teachers with anything they need. Do they?

Fortunately, many of our students do manage to dress appropriately. Some, however, feel the need to dress as if they were an undercover student or as if nothing is left to the imagination. Perhaps they want to relive their high school experiences at a more sophisticated level. Whatever the reason, they create a problem for the mentor teacher, the students, and for us.

Occasionally, we will receive an email or phone call about a student whose sense of fashion is divergent from school policy. The results in a phone conversation between one of us and the candidate, or we schedule a meeting with them. After their initial surprise (really?), they usually agree to dress in a more mature and professional manner. More often, the mentor teacher or school principal meets with the candidate to remind them of the school's dress policy. That usually takes care of the problem.

Helping the teachers depends on the relationship established between the teacher candidate and the supervising mentor teacher. Most of the time, if the candidate makes a good impression and is willing to offer help, the teacher is glad to accept. Occasionally, a candidate is paired with a teacher who feels like the teacher candidate is only in the class to observe. Even if help is offered, it may be declined. These situations can be very frustrating for candidates. If they come to us for help, we do what we can to encourage the teacher to accept the candidate's offer of assistance.

Many times we learn that the teacher has had a bad experience with a teacher candidate in the past and is hesitant to try again. In these situations, we ask that they accept a minimum amount of help from the candidate initially and work up to more involvement if that is successful. Ultimately, the class is the responsibility of the classroom teacher and our candidates are guests there. We have to respect that. Teacher candidates who are committed to the experience, to the students they observe, and to assisting the mentor teacher in any way they can usually have a great experience and find friends and resources that are invaluable tools to help them become better teachers.

In a few cases, the mentor teacher simply does not want help from the teacher candidate or is unwilling to turn over his or her classroom. In these cases, we encourage the candidate to respect the teacher's opinion and to take opportunities to get to know other teachers in the building and learn from them. We keep in touch with the candidate, and if their experience is not benefitting them, we may remove them from the class and place them with another mentor teacher.

Mentor teachers, like teacher candidates, have different personalities. We are lucky in our profession to have a wealth of professionals who want to help our students on their road to becoming teachers. When we occasionally encounter teachers who do not share this desire to contribute, we do not continue to place candidates with them.

One thing most of our teacher candidates learn is that being prepared means preparing for anything from knowledge about the curriculum to how to handle a sick, injured, or angry child. Their time in the classroom is an eye-opening experience on the variety of skills that teachers are expected to utilize in addition to educating their students.

3. RELATE AND COLLABORATE

The first and most important relationship field experience students must form is the relationship with their supervising mentor teacher. This relationship sets the tone for the entire semester.

We are fortunate to have partnership schools with experienced teachers who have supervised students many times. They are experts at helping students establish a relationship of trust and encouragement. Whether this relationship is maintained over the course of the semester is dependent on the attitude and commitment of the teacher candidate.

We are also continuously searching for more mentor teachers due to increasing numbers of student interns and to avoid overloading the mentors who are already helping us. Unfortunately, many times these new placements are at the mercy of administrative personnel who are not located at the schools and who are out of touch with the faculty in the school.

Sometimes the principal of the school insists on making the assignments and personalities and experience are not always priorities. In situations like this, we try to keep the lines of communication open with the mentor teachers and the candidates. We make sure both have all the information necessary about the requirements and needs for the field placement.

WELCOME FOR PRACTICUM MENTORS/SUPERVISING TEACHERS

Thank you for agreeing to supervise one of our Master of Arts in Teaching students for their practicum experience. The student was provided an orientation at the beginning of the semester where the assignments for practicum were explained. The student should have given you a letter that lists those requirements so you will know what is expected of them.

We stressed at orientation that they exhibit professionalism when they are in the school. They were advised to address all staff in a professional manner, dress professionally, and conduct themselves as a professional with both staff and students. I hope they assimilated this information. If they did not, please feel free to contact me.

I realize that supervising/mentoring a student or new teacher is an additional task added to an already long list of things you do as an educator. I appreciate you for taking it on. The information you give our student will be valuable to them because they will be able to see how the content they have previously learned is used in the field.

If you have any questions about the assignments or what you are supposed to do, please feel free to contact me via email (____) or my office phone (____), and I will respond as soon as I can. If you feel you need to contact me about a problem or question that needs a more immediate response, you can reach me at my cell number (____). The students do not have this number.

> I hope you have a good experience with our student and they are a benefit to you and your class during this semester. Thank you for sharing your expertise.

Sometimes, if we are lucky, we end up with a great new mentor teacher. Sometimes we are able to establish a working relationship that is okay, but not ideal. Occasionally, we find that we need to remove the teacher candidate and find another placement. We have heard comments from candidates who received placements with these new mentors that they saw issues during their field experiences that helped them to understand the importance of the methods and procedures we taught them in classes.

For candidates who are able to maintain a good relationship with their supervising teachers, there is an added benefit: collaboration. College instructors can tell candidates about the benefits of collaboration, but until they have an opportunity to collaborate with another professional in the public school, they have no concept of its power. This is where the true benefit of field experiences can be seen. It is one of the reasons that supervising teachers continue to give their time to teacher candidates learning the art of teaching.

Field placement can be an enlightening experience for candidates who come from small communities if their placement is in an urban area. Working with children who have different abilities is something they have some familiarity with. Working with students who have different cultural backgrounds, races, and ethnic backgrounds can be more challenging. To add to the difficulty, many candidates doing field experience are not in the classroom every day. They do not get to know the students like the classroom teacher gets to know them. The classroom teacher can guide them in relating to these students by encouraging them to work with the students and by modeling the importance of establishing a good relationship with students.

Many of our candidates learn a new appreciation of the skills teachers develop in managing classrooms and students. A few candidates question their ability to teach these students. The value of field experience is the opportunity for teacher candidates to experience authentic experiences in the classroom.

4. ESSENTIAL COMMUNICATION—NOT INCLUDING TEXTING AND SOCIAL MEDIA

One of the first things we learn when dealing with teacher candidates and mentor teachers during field experience is the importance of communication. Initially in our classes, we focus on correct grammar in oral and written communication and on using appropriate language. During orientation, we emphasize the importance of communicating with mentor teachers. We remind them never to assume their mentor knows why they are not at school or what their requirements are. It is the teacher candidate's job to keep the mentor informed. We have quickly learned that this is only the tip of the communication iceberg.

"Ask first" should be written on an easily visible space on every teacher candidate's body. In spite of orientation information, stories of previous experiences, and constant reminders, each semester we send students to the field who assume the schools know what their requirements are, and the school should and will take responsibility for all deadlines. Teacher candidates take advantage of materials the mentor has prepared and decide to take a look at them without asking. They do not seem to realize that this can be seen as an invasion of their mentor's space or can be a liability issue for the mentor and for the school.

One semester, we received a call from a teacher after the candidate's first visit to her room. According to the mentor, the candidate arrived after class had begun, and the mentor instructed her to sit at her desk. While the mentor was teaching the lesson, the candidate looked through materials on her desk including a notebook that contained personal information about her students. The mentor requested that we remove the teacher candidate from her class. She said she could not work with her if the candidate did not understand the importance of confidentiality and liability.

We apologized and removed the teacher candidate. When we informed the candidate she was being removed from her placement, she was amazed. She had no concept of the seriousness of her actions. Needless to say, we worked on a plan to help her understand the importance of privacy, confidentiality, and respect for others property. Ask first.

Teaching is not a game, and middle or high school students are not peers. Unfortunately, many candidates want to be that "nice teacher" — the students' friend. What they do not realize is that "friending" students on social media lets them into your personal space. All of it.

Information shared on social media is not appropriate to share with students. How do we know? Of course they have done it. We have received calls from teachers who are dealing with parents who saw things on social media that teacher candidates have posted. Do they forget that students are seeing this information? We think it may be more that they are so used to sharing information through social media that it never occurs to them that some of their "friends" should not be able to see everything they do in their lives, including partying, boozing it up, and needing to put on more clothing.

Their response when we call them in to discuss the problem is almost always amazement. This is generally followed by, "Why is this a problem? I was only trying to be their friend!"

How do you get this point across to the teacher candidate? One teacher at a conference we attended shared that she used her class list every semester and pulled information from social media shared by several of her students. She created a slideshow with the information and then showed it to the class. After the slideshow, she went over the importance of editing information that is available to the students. Did it have an impact? The teacher told us that students were shocked at the information she was able to obtain about them on social media. Many of them sought her out to counsel them on taking information down or unsubscribing from social media.

An especially difficult concept for teacher candidates is the teacher–student relationship. Many of our candidates are not much older than the high school students they teach. They try to relate to them on a level that is more of a friend than an adult or authority figure. What they forget is that friendship comes with expectations that, many times, a teacher candidate cannot meet. This leads to misunderstandings and hurt feelings on the side of the student.

Other candidates go to the opposite extreme. They are so concerned about being the authority figure that they come across as autocratic and unapproachable to the students. This leads to behavior issues that impact the ability of the teacher candidate to teach and of the students to learn. An experienced mentor with a good relationship with the class and with the university is worth their weight in gold in situations like this. They can help guide the candidate in finding that balance needed to establish authority while encouraging the students that their classrooms are safe and their opinions are important.

WHAT IS THE SOLUTION? OUR AHA! MOMENTS

I wish we could say we have found the secret to foreseeing every possible problem that pairing a teacher candidate with an experienced mentor teacher might involve. That would be like saying we found Blackbeard's treasure. We have discovered some successful techniques and are building on them in our constant search for the ideal field experience. Some of our successes include:

- Establishing strong partnerships with diverse urban and suburban schools in our area.
- Creating a cohort of strong mentor teachers who are comfortable with our students and in sharing their ideas for improving our field experiences.
- Establishing relationships with rural schools in locations all over the state that are near where our students live. We try to place our students in locations that involve less than an hour of travel from their homes. Because our students come from locations around the state, we have worked with schools that would not normally be within the range of our university. In these efforts, we have become

familiar with a variety of teachers and new programs that have helped us to expand our knowledge of best practices and creative scheduling for students in a variety of educational settings.
- Creating orientation presentations that effectively cover requirements for field experience and professional behavior that troubleshoot a lot of problems that have previously occurred. Do we cover every problem? No. New problems arise each semester with each new placement location and each new group of students. However, we have managed to cover a sufficient number of possible problems to minimize the number of situations that occur. Each semester gets better as our partnerships get stronger.
- Creating a reporting system for colleagues in higher education so disposition issues that occur in initial classes can be identified and addressed before the candidate is sent into the field.
- Support the public schools that accommodate our candidate placements by keeping the lines of communication open and acting on any problems that might occur quickly and effectively.
- Providing lists of requirements for the candidates that they can bring into the schools to provide administrators and mentor teachers with the information needed to efficiently plan their time together so it does not conflict with the needs of their class.
- Keeping in mind that field partnerships between mentor teachers and candidates are a delicate balance that must be carefully planned and nurtured throughout the semester.
- Diligently working to make certain that schools realize the value they provide for our teacher candidates and our programs by offering and sharing the resources that we can provide to help them improve and continue to offer excellence in education.

THREE

Different Perspectives and Different Players

"All the world's a stage, and all the men and women merely players" comes to mind when I think of the diverse and dynamic world of field placement (William Shakespeare, *As You Like It*, scene 7, 139–43). We have spent many years, decades, pondering the cliché, finding an evolving meaning in these words, especially when it comes to education. Let's face it. We are all performers, and show after show, we perform—our titles dictating our roles.

PLAYERS AND PERFORMANCE: THE ULTIMATE PRODUCTION

Roles often change depending on location. At the university, you could wear one mask, performing the role as instructor and field placement coordinator; likewise, in the public schools, you need a costume change, playing a role as a supporter and encourager. Think about it.

Years ago, we heard a story about a conference presenter who greeted his teacher participants at the door of the conference room. As each participant walked in, he grouped them, seemingly indiscriminately. Once all teachers were seated, he revealed that he had grouped them by the levels they taught: elementary, middle, and secondary. Oddly, he never asked them nor did they have any identifiers that would have given that information away. He then said he could prove it and conducted a quick show of hands, and much to the surprise of the group, he managed to get everyone labeled correctly.

Once the teacher hysteria died down, the teacher shared information about his miraculous method. He said that each teacher plays the role and assumes the appearance of the culture of the level they teach. As the story continued, he even jested that the middle-level teachers were the easiest to spot as they were the wildest, craziest-looking pack in the group. (Allow me to confess, I spent fourteen years in middle level, and I must totally agree.)

Although this tale may be the stuff of urban legends, it carries with it a connection to Shakespeare's earlier words—we are all players, and we mostly gravitate to our roles and conform to them well.

From the university to the school, we all seem to fall in line with the expectations of the roles we play. Depending on where we are and whom we are with, we can experience and inflict infectious positive energy and outcomes, or we can conform to the complacencies and dissonance that oftentimes accompanies our field. With so many variables in the works, is it any wonder that forming partnerships and alliances is so cumbersome?

One mishap with a rogue intern can seal the fate of a superficial partnership. A scorned mentor can scorch the hallway of a school, shutting down once-viable placement options. What happens when an administrator develops a distaste for a supervisor or the university as a whole? How does this animosity impact our partnership and, ultimately, our students? How do we please every player, especially when the players are always changing? From a change of location to a change of mind, field placement coordinators are always working in a system in flux.

With so many vested players involved in the production of teacher education, field placement coordinators must not only be aware of the players, but we must also acknowledge motives, needs, and wants, ultimately using what is in the best interests of students as our litmus test for successful placements and partnerships.

We produce hits, and, occasionally, we produce flops, but despite the outcomes, the play must go on. It is through our deep-rooted connections, where all players have a vested interest in the successful production, that we can create authentic field opportunities and have a meaningful, real impact on all students.

Partnerships thrive on solid relationships that put students front and center. Considering all the different people who are involved in making a successful partnership, creating the synergy that is desperately needed is not always easy. To be honest, it is a struggle that field placement coordinators face daily. Knowing the players and having key insights to the production are necessary to ensure students have the ultimate experience while exploring the field.

As we work through the various players and how they impact our partnerships, keep in mind that the focus is on their impact on field placements and partnerships.

INTRODUCING THE PLAYERS

Kindergarten through Twelfth-Grade Students

If you are in the business of teacher education, the kindergarten through twelfth-grade students are ultimately the customers. They are the playgoers. Every facet of what we design and implement must place their interests at the epicenter of everything we do. When designing field for university students, we cannot lose sight that when we are talking to the public schools, attempting to sell them on a field opportunity, our first obligation must be to the kindergarten through twelfth-grade students.

All too often, we neglect this element. In my dealings with several schools, I find myself on delicate ground when approaching them regarding our university students and teacher education candidates and determining how to be mutually beneficial. Some of these schools have been drop zones for universities where the school was left cleaning up messes and, once again, the kindergarten through twelfth-grade kids paid the price. No longer can we expect schools to keep our students and candidates, training and mentoring them while we kick back, reaping the benefits.

When kindergarten through twelfth-grade students are the focus of our efforts, our university students, candidates, administration, and supervisors will support such an initiative. Ultimately, this is what it is all about—educating students. Another benefit that the students experience when we make our university presence known as a supportive entity is that we pave the way for those kindergarten through twelfth-grade students who have never experienced a vision of higher education for themselves for whatever reason. When our students show up, they inspire those students in a way that we cannot, and they plant a seed of hope in a future that many kindergarten through twelfth-grade students may not have dreamed possible.

Last semester, a call was received from a director at one of our field sites. Fortunately, this was a good call. She wanted to share with us that several university students were continuing to come to the field site to assist the high-poverty, high-need students, despite the fact that these university students had actually fulfilled their requirements. Further, she exclaimed that one of our university football players brought tickets for a game for the kids, creating such a joy for the center. This young man made a difference, a lasting difference, and inspired a vision of higher education for every student he encountered. Our university students develop relationships that ultimately foster our partnership relationships.

University Students and Teacher Education Candidates

Next on our list of most important players are our university students and teacher education candidates. On the stage, they serve in various capacities, from following scripts to stepping out with impromptu moments. They join us as players, and their roles are vital to the production. Some performances may be total perfection while others may suffer from a number of issues. Where one may sing the most melodious tune, another's voice may crack. One may forget his or her lines while another may slip into a fog and forget necessary screen directions. Nonetheless, we are all players and school is the stage.

Some may question this hierarchy. As a matter of fact, some will totally disagree; however, if you are working in teacher education, there is no doubt as to whom we are ultimately serving. By examining our programs and ensuring they ultimately meet the needs of the kindergarten through twelfth-grade students, we are equipping our students and candidates to teach—which is paramount. We are in a service industry, and we are not the ones being served. This requires a total paradigm shift, especially when those occasional entitled university students show up ready to be served. Changing the culture to be a support structure for the public schools will be a challenge when expecting university students and even teacher candidates to sacrifice time in the field.

First, the field must mean something. Our university students and teacher candidates need to see and experience the authenticity. The earlier example of university students continuing to serve in a field where their time was up is a classic example of a field that extended their own purposes. Each sought to make a difference and was provided with a field opportunity that allowed them to do so. Showing up with football tickets was great, but just the simple act of showing up beyond requirement took initiative that was rooted in opportunity.

Also, university students and teacher candidates want university supervisors and instructors present, serving alongside them in the field. Not only does research of best field practices tell us this, but our students also tell us this.

In both the graduate and undergraduate programs, we have reading lab classes. In evaluations over the past year, students in these classes have raved about us being with them, serving and modeling best practices. When teaching the same course without the lab element, before partnerships and summer experiences were created, reviews were not as positive. Although our students appreciated the strategies shared and experienced our passion for differentiating and reaching all learners, especially struggling readers, they failed to see the significance. They never got the real purpose.

On the contrary, students in courses enriched with lab, where we worked directly with kindergarten through twelfth-grade students, were extremely complimentary and gracious for the experience. Several commented that the class was one of the most important ones they had taken. A few requested that the course be offered an entire year, and some inquired as to other courses in our programs that had similar lab-based opportunities. Why?

While we would love to step back and say it was because we are super dynamic and wonderful teachers, we know better. Our first offerings of this course proved that—before the lab piece was implemented. The success is in the field where instructors are present, modeling, and guiding. Being present for the kindergarten through twelfth-grade students is a responsibility, but guiding teacher candidates is a priority. There were numerous times when our students have needed assistance with the administration of literacy assessments and interventions, and, fortunately, we were right there to assist them.

Instead of disgruntled students harping about one more thing to do and no real model to follow, our students looked forward to our sessions. After each lab, we reflect, and these reflections continue to guide our practice and instruction. From our strengths and weakness to our kindergarten through twelfth-grade students' needs, we curtailed our instruction, informed by all our students' current needs, creating a truly student-centered course.

Putting students first means also keeping them informed. Throughout this book, you will be given lots of great ideas to keep your students apprised; however, two tools that have revolutionized communication are GroupMe and REMIND 101. These apps are a great go-to when it comes to communicating with students. These texting—now chat option—tools allow mentors to schedule and send announcements and important reminders. It even allows students to contact teachers or mentors via text, providing instant support for students in the field. Why is this so important? Between questions that students may have to concerns they encounter in the field, we are on call, twenty-four/seven. Students and candidates travel all over the place, and we do our very best to be there for them whenever a situation may arise. These apps have quickly become our main source for communication and support for students and candidates.

Our focus must be on the students—again, *all* students. Each student we work with brings value to the field, and we owe it to each and every student to nurture and meet them where they are. It is not always easy and it requires that each encounter, no matter the circumstance, must be handled with care. At the end of the day, we are all in this together.

Working with university students and teacher candidates, we are reminded of the important role we all play in relation to one another. No role is complete without the other. We know that our students and candidates need total support, that village model, where we all take responsibility for their growth, success, and even failures; however, we are also the benefactors of their gifts and talents. We have so much to learn from our teachers of tomorrow, and knowing that we are all connected—one community of players—makes the investment of our time and energy worth the sacrifice.

Mentors and Classroom Teachers

Are mentors and classroom teachers the same? Yes and no. Classroom teachers are teachers who serve kindergarten through twelfth-grade students and may or may not work with our students or teacher candidates; however, we included them because they play a role in our placements, and they influence other players. Classroom teachers who are not assigned as mentors often serve as secondary resources to our students and candidates. Their influence can never be overlooked, especially when it comes to the public school setting. We want their support, especially for our candidates. For the most part, they are a beacon of hope and assistance to our students and candidates, reaching out to them and guiding them through the complicated school maze. However, there are those who are anything but beacons of hope.

An example of a classroom teacher serving as a player in this production—the court jester—happened our first year as field placement coordinators. We had a candidate who suffered from a classic case of TMI (too much information). Her mentor was treated to a rundown of our candidate's history and issues, from relationships to medications and medical concerns, our well-meaning candidate put it all out there. Some may think that this was ethically responsible; however, within a week, she dominated lunchtime conversations with her opinions and thoughts, rubbing other teachers the wrong way, as one could imagine.

One particular teacher got cornered in the hallway one day and was treated to a full-on theatrical production. Needless to say, following this awkward encounter, the classroom teacher, not the mentor, managed to share and even elaborated on some details with anyone who would listen to the story of the crazy intern. Talk of a crazy intern finally made its way to the university, and before we knew it, we had a real issue in the making. Who would have thought someone removed from our placement practices could have such tremendous impact on our candidates?

With that said, we refer to teachers who actually guide our students or candidates in the field as mentors. Like Merlin to Arthur, a mentor plays a crucial role in the development of the mentee. Consider your own walks in new venues. Even now, we seek out mentors to guide and advise us when we're facing new experiences. Seeking the wisdom and expertise of the wiser, more experienced sage is natural to those of us who truly want to learn and excel in our respective areas. Mentor teachers do more than model lessons for our candidates; they reveal the secrets of teaching and open doors of understanding, providing a path of learning from content to pedagogy. Likewise, they have scaled the lands before our candidates, mapping the rugged terrain, serving as pioneers to the teachers who will follow in their footsteps.

These mentors have an agreement with the university to serve, guide, and support our students and candidates while supervising our students who are in the field, and most do exactly so, going above and beyond the call to ensure our candidates have the very best experience possible.

We've learned that there is no secret formula to matching mentors and candidates (i.e., interns). Quite frankly, we have had wonderful mentors struggle with a particular intern, and we have had average teachers serve as exemplar mentors. Each semester, new variables surface making determining a perfect match quite cumbersome. For example, we have worked with an incredible mentor the past five years. Her guidance has paved the way for numerous candidates entering the classroom. Her reviews are excellent, and her candidates praise her character and her pedagogy. Both male and female candidates were overly impressed and motivated by this stellar mentor. However, this past semester marked a challenge for this amazing mentor as she experienced a candidate who not only challenged her but also was not the picture of passion and perfection when it comes to teaching.

There were no red flags with this particular candidate. Her grades were good; she passed all the tests. Nothing about this candidate's disposition suggested there were any credible concerns; however, within a few weeks at the site, issues were mounting. From promptness to professional discourse, this candidate's rap sheet was building, and along with her indiscretions, the candidate was steadily challenging the mentor's patience.

Frustrated, the mentor decided to take a different approach, and instead of nurturing the candidate, she decided brutal honesty was the best policy. This resulted in several lectures and heated discussions between the mentor and the candidate. Consequently, the candidate was in tears, claiming that the mentor was downright hostile toward her and had created an environment of fear. Finally, things had escalated to the point of no return. After a conference with all the players where conversations became heated and solutions were nowhere in sight, it was determined the candidate needed to be removed.

For the most part, our mentors are ready for these "black swans," the unexpected; however, we are seeing more and more students who do not always respect the mentor and his or her experience, making the black swans a new norm. The Millennial Express has pulled into the station, and aboard this passenger train are black swans entering this exciting profession called teaching, and preparing mentors for this new wave is a real challenge that we are all facing. Training our mentors is vital to ensure we are ready for the future.

Each semester, we host a meet and greet. At this event, we enjoy lunch with our mentors, supervisors, program coordinators, university faculty, and our candidates. This is an opportunity for everyone to meet and plan prior to the beginning of the semester, and with so many of our active players involved in this function, we ensure everyone is hearing the same information, leaving little room for misunderstandings. After a working lunch, we have breakout sessions—one for our mentors, supervisors, and coordinators, and one for our candidates. This is an opportunity for our mentors to ask questions and hear from others who have mentored before. It is collaboration at its finest, and the turnout is incredible.

Mentors must be "in the know." From coming to the university for a meet and greet to our onsite visits, we establish rapport as early as possible and maintain that rapport throughout the semester. First, our web page is a tool. Housed on our web page are calendars, handbooks, assignments, and rubrics—every tool our supervisors, candidates, and mentors will need throughout the process of internship. Our mentor handbook, for example, outlines expectations of supervisors, interns, and mentors, leaving no one in the dark regarding duties. Our web page sets the stage for transparency.

We have several other mechanisms that keep the mentor momentum rolling. For example, a sometimes-overlooked tool we use is email. Sounds simple, but it is anything but simple. Not only are we as the field coordinators checking in, but supervisors and program coordinators are also reaching out, offering assistance and advice throughout the mentoring process. We have a real system of keeping communication ongoing, and mentors love it.

Google Forms is a game-changing tool. Each semester, surveys are sent asking mentors to rate their candidate's supervisor, as well as inquiring about their experience, their intern, our performance, and any suggestions or comments. This survey has become a great source of inspiration and learning, and will lead to innovations in how we view mentor training. Currently, we are in the process of designing an interactive mentor training (online) based on the results of this survey. Believe it or not, we have so much to learn from these mentors. Consider this. They are not only mentoring our students; they are likewise mentoring us.

Regardless of how you value your mentors, know this: they are the backbone of field placement. Recruitment of quality mentors must be a priority if we are going to ensure best field practices, especially when it comes to our university students and candidates.

District-Level Administration

For most of us in field placement, we know that there are certain hoops we have to jump through. District-level administration is one of those hoops. Some districts require that district-level contact must be made prior to even requesting a placement in a school. Most of our district-level administrators are quick to heed the call, serving as those very necessary investors that make a production even possible; however, there are district-level administrators who we struggle with when it comes to communication.

Every semester, we send placement requests, the earlier the better. Instantly, we get responses. As these confirmations roll in, we begin building Google spreadsheets and we share this spreadsheet with our students as a notification system of placements being fulfilled. Each week, we have gaps where district-level administrators have yet to get back to us. After a month, we resend emails. After a few months, we're on the phone. We jokingly call ourselves "school stalkers." Sadly, it is true.

Why is this lapse of communication so frustrating? After months of waiting, we may get denied, and by that time, we are competing to get our students and candidates in the field. It is beyond frustrating, and it could be totally prevented. Knowing we have these district-level administrators out there, we now follow up earlier and begin reaching out sooner to prevent months of lapses; however, it still happens, and it is always frustrating.

The reality is that we are not the most important priority of a district- or building-level administrator. As a matter of fact, we are nowhere near the top of the heap. Every email we send, we know we're adding another job to the growing list of jobs administrators have. We get it, but it doesn't change the fact that we all have jobs to do, and, unfortunately, our job depends on others doing theirs. This is the harsh reality of field placement. Our hands are sometimes tied as we attempt, repeatedly, to jump through those moving hoops.

We would love to end it here and say that communication is the only real concern involving this player; however, it is not. Policies are constantly arising, and with them, changes beckon. We frequently have to monitor and adjust when it comes to assignments, report dates, signing in procedures, mentor communication, and many other protocols based on district-level initiatives.

For example, our candidates all report on different dates to their field site at the beginning of each semester based on district preferences. Some districts, preferring interns not be privy to certain professional developments, have forbidden their presence on campuses until professional developments are completed, while others see the value in their being present and want them at everything. This is a real concern, and this type of thinking is hard to combat as a candidate coming from the university and being viewed as the outsider.

District-level administrators have the power and influence to change this type of exclusionary practices, yet they often fall short when it comes to advocating for teacher education creating issues of our own making.

Again, "we are they" is a philosophy preached by many but followed by few.

Working together is the only way to ensure that the ultimate goal of kindergarten through twelfth-grade student achievement is met. Investors in teacher education are desperately needed. Advocates are needed, and we need district-level administrators to get on board, because when they work with us instead of against us, truly, great productivity and innovation in teacher education are possible.

School Building Administration

Without the support of excellent, supportive school building administration, all is for naught. In the schools where communication is flowing and encouraging, we have some amazing experiences taking place. Principals who work with us and support our students and candidates are leaders who see the value and understand the importance of working together. They are the heart of the production, the stage manager. Without their efforts and vision, there would be no happy ending.

For the past three years, we have worked with a middle-level administrator who is a champion for education for all students. She gets it. Her school is a cohort campus where we send groups of our middle-level candidates, and her teachers, under her incredibly supportive guidance, mentor and manage our students and candidates. They are invested. When they suffer, we suffer. When they have a need, we try to fill it. When we have a need, the school is responsive and supportive.

Although this school is over twenty miles from our campus, we host an onsite tutoring program (two days a week) for children who are in foster care within this district. Our university students serve this site, receiving specialized training for working with these students. All the while, caring for our candidates are teachers who truly appreciate our efforts. They get it.

Undoubtedly, the building leader is the visionary. His or her leadership has made this partnership a success. We work in other great buildings with great administrators, but this is on an entirely different level. There is a synergy within this school that breeds excellence in teaching and learning. This is truly a learning organization, seeking to learn, inspire, and give back. Our students and candidates are experiencing school at its very best, and this is largely due to the leadership in place.

When leadership is lacking, struggles are not only seen, but they are likewise experienced. From micromanaging administrators to controlling administrators, we have sampled several styles, but have still found common ground. Administrators are not all created equal; they have different skill sets and gifts, and before we get frustrated and give up, we always try to be sensitive to the issues that administrators face every day. Their job is not an easy one, and, again, we are not the most important job on their to-do list. A cranky administrator does not equate a loss. For the most part, we can make it work; however, cooperation may not always be possible.

We have worked with schools that have experienced frequent administrator turnovers, and morale in these buildings is not good. When administration creates a dead zone culture, we have a real problem. The spirit of the school is zapped, and teachers have very little to give. Being aware of this climate is crucial when it comes to field placement.

We do not want our candidates in fields of flux or attempted mutinies. Imagine a school full of the revolutionaries of teaching, armed with torches and pitchforks. Yes, there are growing pains that come with teacher education, but we must seek effective, sound leaders and buildings where our students have a possibility of thriving. Throwing them into a scene of *Pirates of the Caribbean* is inviting more troubles than any of us want to battle. They are not plank-walking ready! How do we discover this? Listen.

First, teachers talk. We cannot help it. Building those mentor relationships will pay off in the long run. Also, our students and candidates will reveal information and have insights as well. Assignments that are attached to the field experiences must include opportunities for candid feedback. Reflections or journals may provide a conduit for conversation; however, we seek our students and candidates out, face-to-face. Many of them have been burned by putting things in writing; therefore, they need an opportunity to talk with supervisors and field placement coordinators without the fear of retribution. This is where we make impactful discoveries. From the mentors to our students, pictures begin to come into view, and the insights we gain from these players allow us to make informed decisions regarding placements.

Rarely have we had to pull from a school because of poor administration; however, it has happened, especially when changes are always on the horizon in some districts, and teacher morale resembles *The Walking Dead*. Being aware and having solid relationships in buildings will prove invaluable when it comes to making decisions that have a lasting impact on our students and candidates.

University Administration, Supervisors, and Faculty

There are so many players within the university setting that we decided to group them all together because their names may differ, but, in essence, we share many similarities when it comes to working in the schools. We stand on stage and assume our roles. Many of us fall into this category too well and are not always received well when it comes to the public schools where the rubber meets the road. How many times have we heard that a professor or a supervisor is out of touch? Too many to recount. (When discussing university administration within one school, we actually heard the words, "Do they ever leave the ivory tower long enough to experience what it is they teach?") Harsh words, but this is the image we have to reframe.

Administration is needed to do what we do. They produce our production. Without their investment, the show is off. We cannot move forward with innovative field opportunities without the support of a visionary administration. It simply cannot happen. We need the support of administration and their ultimate understanding, especially when we spend more time in the field than we do at the university. They must see and experience that value, and when they do, their support will give wings to authentic field practices.

Faculty who work with our students and candidates must dust off their costumes and prepare themselves for performance. Your presence in the field is requested. Why? How can you teach to a field in which you cannot relate? Sorry to tell you, but you are not relevant without field practice. Your street credibility is trending down every year you are out of the classroom, and if you work in any way to prepare future teacher educators, you should be in the field.

Assignments should match opportunities that are birthed from course objectives, and without gracing the field with your presence, how do you really know? When your students see you in the field, serving alongside them, you reframe their view. When mentors or school administrators see you in the field, working with their students, you reframe their view. With all of this reframing, thriving partnerships are possible.

Supervisors are building relationships every time they grace a building with their presence, serving as ambassadors. Most of our supervisors are faculty first, so the faculty lecture applies here too. You are in the field, but are you working in the field? Are you reaching out when you visit schools or are you in and out, avoiding bells and students? We had a mentor this last semester actually say, "I saw the supervisor, but he never once spoke to me. He was always in a rush and never made time for me." Never do we want our presence to be viewed as a concern or a nuisance. We had a supervisor who actually reprimanded a mentor for lacking a classroom management plan. Without a relationship and without a clue, a supervisor made a quick judgment based on bad information. Call in the firemen!

Thankfully, most of our supervisors are seen as real support systems. Students and mentors trust them because they know their stuff and because they value the field, and everyone knows it. Because of their intricate knowledge of mentors and students, we rely heavily on their expertise for placement requests. They are the eyes and ears in the schools and in the classrooms. Not only do they know their programs, but also they are experts in curriculum and they have detailed knowledge of mentors within their disciplines and the students they teach. Without our relationship with supervisors, we would blindly make some placements and the detriment of our candidates.

Having honest dialogue with administration, faculty, supervisors, and other university key players makes a difference. When issues arise, being able to discuss concerns candidly with faculty and supervisors without fear of offense is very important. When we all work together, ensuring the best experience for our students—again, weaving a field that is authentic and meaningful—all students are the ultimate beneficiaries.

University Field Placement

We are the directors, casting and creating a production that begets other productions. We have a foot on the stage and a foot in the audience and are the servant to many masters. Behind the scenes, we are promoting and preparing, and during production, we are never still. Field placement is one of the toughest, most important jobs in colleges of education, and without a doubt, it is the most rewarding.

Being in the field, if you are a teacher by heart, is where you find your joy. When we enter a school and see our students, we are reminded of why we do what we do. It is for students—all students. Throughout our work with the various players, it always comes back to students; however, we still have a job to do.

From seeking requests to filling requests, we are always on call. Emails are a constant, and we find ourselves responding or composing incessantly. Training students and candidates along with mentors and supervisors is our job. If a situation happens, we do not want our students or candidates to be unprepared. Meeting with partners and recruiting mentors is always occurring. These meetings result in more work and emails. Putting out an occasional fire is just part of the job. This can take an hour or a few days and normally comes from out of nowhere. Preparing a semester, even a year, ahead of the production is necessary to ensure a successful production.

We should have a checklist, and we should constantly be checking and adding to the checklist. Networking. Networking. (Did I mention networking?) Meetings are the norm because field placement is involved in every aspect of the college of education. We bring a perspective and advocacy that is always needed when decisions regarding students are being made.

There are other players in this production, from support staff to community partners, yet these highlighted players are vital to fieldwork. An issue with one player can impact several other players, causing a rainstorm of troubles. Likewise, a success with one player can influence other players, creating a multitude of opportunities. We must be mindful of these connections and our own roles within the production.

One mishap with a building-level administrator can impact our relationship with an entire district, and it doesn't end there. District connections and ties span across the state we live in—a mishap in one district will be known in another, just as one supervisor who goes above and beyond in one school can positively impact the relationship with a district, opening the door to opportunities.

Players and their attitudes matter. Based on what we have shared, we could throw our hands up and give up, but we choose to focus on the positive and the incredible impact we make in the lives of students. As we write this book, we know that next year will herald in many stressful situations and changes; however, our attitudes make a difference. From the university to the schools, when students are the focus and our efforts and agendas are in line with their best interests, good things happen. We want to be a part of something magical—the Broadway production equivalent of *The Lion King*. Every semester presents new opportunities, and, players, we set the stage.

FOUR
Can You Be Proactive?

Proactive. Preparing for or intervening in an expected occurrence or situation—especially one that is negative or difficult. To anticipate. Being proactive is vital to safety when battling a structure fire and to the successful growth of this year's perennials when tending to a garden. Many things are put into place, preparations are made, and rewards and consequences are considered when being proactive. Working with teacher candidates through their field experiences requires the skills of a stealth fire brigade, a master gardener, and a dynamic educator—skills we continuously shape, mold, and perfect.

Having strong, established structures in place in order to be proactive rather than reactive is one of the hallmarks of our success and is necessary unless you want to go up in a blaze on scene. Building a sound infrastructure conducive for teacher candidate growth and development ensures success for the future teachers they will become.

This well-built infrastructure will ensure that even when the occasional fire breaks out, the structure is still left as a starting point from which to rebuild rather than having to bulldoze all the hard work begun by the university, faculty, and teacher candidate and starting again from ground zero.

DISPOSITIONS: ESTABLISHING EXPECTATIONS

In the Master of Arts in Teaching (MAT) program, being proactive with our teacher candidates begins with new student orientation (appendix A). Program faculty are recruited to speak about the MAT program, Praxis requirements, provisional licensure, academic integrity, being a graduate student, professionalism, field experiences, and more. Outside resources are brought in to share expertise about library resources, licensing requirements, and technology resources. Added bonuses include substitute agencies onsite to recruit for local schools as well as a student panel (alumni and current students) sharing pros, cons, tools for survival while teaching and taking coursework, tips, and answering new student questions.

Proactivity continues into the first class our students take: Analysis and Practice of Teaching. Teacher candidates are introduced to the MAT Dispositions Rubric. For each area being assessed, candidates can score On Target, Proficient/Meets Expectations, Basic/Acceptable, or Unsatisfactory.

Dispositions assessed fall under the following categories:

- Values Learning and Knowledge
- Values Diversity
- Values Collaboration
- Values Professionalism
- Values Personal Integrity

Within each category, specific dispositions are assessed regarding attendance; class preparation; in-class performance; self-reflection; relationships with others; group work; professional development and involvement; resourcefulness; respect for school rules, policies, and norms; communication; emotional control and responsibility; and ethical behavior, including being an appropriate role model.

Guiding teacher candidates through each item on the disposition rubric in the first class of the program helps to ensure understanding before candidates are expected to utilize the rubric to self-assess. This rubric is employed throughout the program—specifically during field experiences and as problems arise.

When faculty experience dispositional issues with MAT students, they refer to the dispositions rubric and submit an accompanying narrative to the MAT coordinator. These are kept in student files, and after at least two separate issues are brought to light, the MAT coordinator and/or department chair visit with the student and develop an improvement plan.

It is always interesting when reviewing the disposition rubric with new MAT teacher candidates. Invariably, students will respond, "Doesn't everyone know these things?" "Isn't this common sense?" "We are in graduate school. Do we really have to be told to show up, be prepared, and be professional?" The answer? In every area on the disposition rubric, we have had at least one teacher candidate score "unsatisfactory." We then share some of the more entertaining stories with our new teacher candidates followed by, "We can't make this stuff up. Common sense is not always common practice."

EARLY FIELD EXPERIENCES: BUILDING A STRONG FOUNDATION

In middle and secondary programs, baby steps are taken so that scaffold teacher candidates can work positively and professionally in schools beginning in early field experiences. This guidance can begin as long as one to two years before the culminating internship experience. For early field in all programs, we embrace the idea of putting our students in the field immediately—beginning with courses even before admission to teacher education. In these early field experiences, students do not just observe. Much like firefighter candidates attending the fire academy, through classes and coursework, the instructor demonstrates or models proper technique then deems the candidate able to perform their duties to ensure they are ready to go out on scene or out into the schools.

Instruction Meets Practice: Middle and Secondary Tutoring Sites

Scaffolding begins with a field experience coordinator attending every class with early field experience to train all students in professional behaviors, general procedures, and working with mentors, supervisors, and students. Technical and physical aspects of navigating field sites are also addressed.

For early field, we have partnered with ten local schools to offer tutoring services for their struggling learners. Because this is a joint effort between the university and school-based tutoring sites, it is important that everyone pitches in and that lines of communication are kept open. Mentors are positioned at each site, and principals and field coordinators are also part of the team—working together to ensure students' success.

Like firefighters doing safety inspections, the field coordinators visit each site periodically. Field coordinators are in contact on a monthly basis with principals and mentors discussing and identifying students who are doing well and students who need interventions to show improvement. These early and immediate experiences are essential so that our students are not just observing but are working with actual children, much like firefighters learning on and working with the actual equipment.

Instruction Meets Practice: Reading Centers

Reading Difficulties is a class in both the middle-level and MAT programs that all preschool through fourth grade and middle-level majors take. In this course, MAT students work with kindergarten through eighth-grade students in our university's Reading Success Center, and middle-level students work onsite with struggling readers. Our programs provide mutual aid to the reading center and local middle school when manpower is so desperately needed due to limited resources.

Teacher candidates assess their assigned kindergarten through eighth-grade student, analyze the results, and design and implement appropriate interventions. Lesson plans must be turned in before working with students in the reading center so the instructor has time to review them, offer feedback, and give the teacher candidate ample time to correct the plans before actual implementation akin to the firefighters who preplan in the event of an incident to ensure a basic attack plan is in place.

The instructor and the reading center director are present at all reading center nights in the MAT program, and the instructor and school staff are present and available during the middle-level class. Through instruction, we are gardeners preparing the soil. Water and fertilizer are provided as needed, either through our presence or assistance. By modeling appropriate assessments and strategies during the reading centers as well as before and after class time, we are aiding in our students' growth by nurturing them.

Not only are our university students plants that need nurturing to grow, but the kindergarten through eighth-grade students we service in these reading centers are also in need. Like tending to a garden, sometimes you find that the plants will not grow. Is it too much or too little sunlight? Is our plan in the wrong location? Do we need a different fertilizer? Is there an ailment we are missing? In this instance, the instructor and teacher candidates work together to help determine if we need to dig deeper, try an alternative strategy, or wait because sometimes it just takes a little longer.

In the past two years, our state has passed a dyslexia law where all teachers are to receive professional development on the markers of dyslexia. This has been a challenge and something that most educators know nothing about. Our reading centers and instructors have been proactive in working with this law and informing our students. This has become a major part of the coursework. Teacher candidates are being prepared and empowered to identify markers of dyslexia and follow that up with specific screeners if warranted.

Several teacher candidates have identified markers of dyslexia in the kindergarten through eighth-grade students they were working with during intervention time. By working with their instructor, the students were able to coadminister a more detailed dyslexia screener, interpret those results, and offer this to parents so the students can also receive needed interventions and services at school. If the instructors were not present and equipped with the knowledge of additional assessment instruments, our students would be left struggling with identifying the true problem and being able to provide the most appropriate intervention. Most important, our teacher candidates leave us with the skills and abilities to offer tier 2 and tier 3 interventions and advocate for their students.

Overall, great success has been experienced in these reading centers, with proactive structures being a great contributor to that success. For students without teaching experience, this is a wonderful first experience in that they are working one-on-one or one-on-two with their instructor present during interventions. During testing time, this is extremely beneficial, as this is the first time for students to give these type of assessments. They often need a gentle reminder on testing procedures and where to go next.

As a class, the students work together afterward to analyze and start finding areas of concern so that students have a direction in writing their lesson plans. Additionally, the instructors model appropriate strategies, which are in turn put into practice in the reading centers so that students are immediately applying what they are learning. Being proactive and present ensures problems, misconceptions, and misunderstandings are immediately addressed before they become larger issues.

Having proactive structures in place to help our teacher candidates while working in the reading centers for their coursework has resulted in many highlights. One kindergarten through eighth-grade student had attended our center for over a year, showing little to no improvement. Our teacher candidate working with her was determined to dig deeper. Sometimes it's not easy to determine a problem quickly, but by utilizing additional screeners, the candidate found strong markers for dyslexia. After starting this student on The Barton Reading Program for Dyslexia, she could read and comprehend a primer-level story for the first time ever. Seeing those moments makes all of the work worthwhile.

However, sometimes the garden needs to be weeded. Frankly, everyone is not cut out to be a teacher. One teacher candidate consistently came to the reading center without a plan, would not work with the instructor to get assistance with planning, and spent her time wandering through books and attempting to read various levels together. After conferencing with this teacher candidate, it was shared that this student was really struggling with what to do. However, she did not want to put the effort in to try and decided that teaching was not for her. It is always sad when any candidate leaves the fold, but if a candidate cannot work one-on-one with a student, we are left asking this: how will you manage and differentiate for an entire classroom?

PRACTICUM AND INTERNSHIP I

In Practicum and Internship I, we strive to be proactive by sending teacher candidates out into a longer field experience but with their protective gear in place. They are equipped with knowledge of coursework, a mentor teacher, and a university supervisor or instructor. Working in tandem and with several other proactive structures place, the goal is to get this teacher candidate ready for internship. It is important to note that not all of the teacher candidates experience traditional practicum and internship placements. Many MAT students have teaching jobs in their own classrooms and therefore get to complete these field experiences in their own classrooms.

Disposition rubrics are addressed in both of these courses. Students self-assess at the beginning of the semester. Mentor teachers assess the students around the middle of the semester and the end of the semester. Copies of the disposition rubrics are sent to university supervisors or the instructor. These are used to catch problems while students are out in the field. Many times mentor teachers do not let us know there are issues until it is too late.

For example, one of our students completed her Practicum and Internship I in a prekindergarten classroom. The student struggled greatly with lesson planning, classroom management, attendance, and respect for the mentor teacher. None of this was communicated to the university supervisor or field placement coordinator. If it had been, a professional development plan or other alternative could have been put in place to assist the student and help make this a more positive experience for the mentor teacher. However, by not finding out until there was one week left in the semester, our hands were tied. Without documentation and giving the student the chance and time to remediate, failure or removal was not an option. This was clearly a student that needed some more work, but the lack of communication from the mentor teacher did not provide the opportunity in a timely manner.

Now that the disposition rubric is in place, we have caught and been able to address immediately, and early in the semester, students who are excessively late, absent because they're on a cruise, beating the buses out of the parking lot to leave, being disrespectful to mentor teachers, and speaking inappropriately to students, such as "You don't like my jacket? Well, your momma liked it last night." Several students we have discovered are on their cell phones and not participating during meetings or when the teacher is teaching. This quick check provides invaluable information.

Mentor teachers observe a lesson in Practicum in the MAT program, setting up a powerful proactive structure. These mentor teachers are the boots on the ground and can keep us apprised of how the teacher candidate is doing and hopefully eliminating the dog and pony shows that are often the case in formal evaluations. Using Danielson's TESS rubric, mentor teachers score all four domains. If a teacher candidate receives a one (out of a possible four) in any area in the TESS rubric, the candidate works with the university instructor to develop a professional growth plan (appendix B). This plan outlines what the university can and will do as well as what the student can and will do to remediate the problem in preparation for Internship. The same is true if a student earns a "C" in Practicum as the MAT program is a graduate course, and students should be earning "As" or "Bs" in graduate work.

Mentor teachers are critical to our work much like training officers are critical to fire departments. On scene, training officers will note what techniques need to be worked on to ensure lives are saved and everybody goes home. Mentor teachers will note what techniques need to be worked on to ensure the intern understands and practices—all children can learn.

The growth plan has been quite successful with our teacher candidates. In one situation, a teacher candidate really struggled in the Practicum and Internship I class and received many ones on the TESS rubric. This could have quickly escalated to a five-alarm fire, but by having these proactive structures in place, an appropriate growth plan was developed. Working with the student, support staff, administrators, MAT coordinator, and university instructor, a thorough and detailed plan was developed to help support this teacher candidate's growth and future success in the program as well as the classroom.

Not only did the program and school take responsibility, but the candidate took responsibility by searching out appropriate professional development to attend as well as professional texts to read and apply what was learned. All were in agreement that our teacher candidate had the capabilities to be a strong teacher; he just needed some additional supports.

INTERNSHIP

Internship is *the* culminating experience in our teacher preparation programs. We have prepared our teacher candidates, put strong support systems in place, and we see how they do when the rubber meets the road. In education, the internship could be likened to that of a probie or firefighter candidate. Teacher candidates are sent out with their full gear and protective clothing. Their captain and lieutenant (mentor teacher and university supervisor) are along for the ride to ensure the candidate has a diverse set of correct tools to use, and they can be provided with additional training or practice on how to use them if necessary.

All students in Internship have a mentor teacher and university supervisor, and this triad work closely together to ensure Internship success. Like a driver/operator of a fire pumper, mentor teachers and university supervisors have to apply the right amount of "pressure" and be there to work alongside the candidate if needed. As in working a pump, if the right amount of pressure and support is not given, the candidate may be unable to wield the hose and keep the classroom flowing and cohesive. Too much or too little could be catastrophic.

At times, there are issues that we know about as the student goes into Internship. In those instances, we can put the teacher candidate under a contract or professional development plan. These can be created for missing or failing Praxis II scores (appendix C), course deficiencies, and/or previous issues that have arisen in early field or Practicum and Internship I. At other times, issues arise during Internship that will require a contract or professional development plan to be put into place (appendices D and E).

The university supervisor and teacher candidate match is like a work of art. We work hard to ensure personalities and teaching/learning styles match. One student really struggled in Practicum and Internship I. She had great difficulties planning lessons, often just copying and pasting from different sources. This candidate struggled with grammar, and she had no confidence in her classroom presence. The candidate and university supervisor were a mismatch. The university supervisor could not see her having a future in teaching, and the candidate always felt the supervisor was out to get her. However, this candidate developed a close relationship with the instructor in one of her courses. The instructor saw something no one else did, and she began nurturing her.

The candidate really blossomed designing interventions and working in the reading center with a struggling reader. Taking her under her wing, the instructor worked diligently with the candidate on her grammar. When it came time for Internship, she was placed in a very specific environment with a specific university supervisor, and they clicked. She received glowing evaluations and became the shining star—a true success story.

At times, it is necessary to call in a Rapid Intervention Team—those on standby whose only job is to go in and rescue their colleagues when the fire becomes too great. In teacher preparation, we have those teams too, only they are our faculty who are ready to go in, observe, offer constructive feedback, model for, and guide them toward improvement.

Even though they're firefighting with the sole purpose of saving the classroom, mentor teacher, and teacher candidate, the gardener inside of them also emerges. These faculty go in daily or weekly if needed to water, fertilize, and nurture the teacher candidate. Sometimes trimming is involved.

One of our students did whatever she wanted for reading instruction and did not utilize district resources or the curriculum map. Quick to yell at the students, it was determined that was her only mode of classroom management. Our Rapid Intervention Team swooped in, directed her toward resources and the curriculum map, modeled some strategies, and strongly advised the yelling as a management strategy to be trimmed from the garden. While this teacher was not successful that semester, after repeating Internship the following semester, she grew leaps and bounds with the Rapid Intervention Team credited for saving the day.

Unfortunately, not all stories have happy endings. Sometimes, no matter who you send in or what you do to be proactive, the placement just does not work. To give you some background, I am not a gardener by nature. I have the brownest thumb of anyone I know. My friends used to joke that if you wanted a plant to die, plant it in Amy's yard. Other friends thought about coming and watering every day—even in the simple things, when it came to gardening, I was not successful. One morning, I found out how bad it really was.

I went to my car to leave for work and noticed a huge hole in my yard. I thought something looked odd about it, so I called my husband down. Lo and behold, a tree was missing. It was the only thing in our yard that hadn't died. Someone came, in the middle of the night, dug that tree up, and took it away. I'm serious. My husband and I finally agreed this was a mercy rescue and imagined that the tree was thriving and growing somewhere else.

I tell the story of the stolen tree because I think it paints the picture perfectly of the struggling teacher candidate. Sometimes, they will not grow or thrive where they are. Sometimes we have to dig them up and plant them in another classroom in order for them to bloom and successfully grow. This happened with one of our candidates.

One of our candidates took internship two times. She was teaching in her own classroom, so we could not just change her placement that semester, but the second time, she changed schools. She dug herself up and planted herself in a different location with our encouragement and advice. This teacher candidate grew leaps and bounds. She was a completely different teacher and successfully graduated after her uprooting.

As in Practicum and Internship I, teacher candidates are scored by their mentor teacher while teaching a lesson using the TESS rubric. The disposition rubric is again utilized. Students self-assess at the beginning and end of the semester. Mentor teachers complete a disposition rubric on the teacher candidates at midterm and the end of the semester. Disposition rubrics are examined to determine any problems that need to be addressed and to ensure the mentor and teacher candidate closely match in their assessment of the dispositions. Furthermore, all teacher candidates placed for internship attend and participate in internship seminars, which are covered in detail in chapter 7.

ADDITIONAL SUPPORTS

Just as firefighters need continued training, refreshers, and additional supports in their line of work, so do our teacher candidates. First and foremost, handbooks are created for mentor teachers, interns, early field students, and supervisors. These are updated at least yearly with the latest programmatic changes and with needs based on previous students and their feedback. These handbooks provide rubrics, assignment due dates, helpful tips, and various other information.

To go with these handbooks, all students go through an orientation the semester before internship and the week that internship starts. Mentor teachers attend or view a virtual orientation each semester, and supervisors attend a meeting that serves as their orientation each semester. All of these provide helpful information to the targeted group, allow time for collaboration and feedback from others with similar experiences, encourage a question and answer time, and review all new updates to the field whether the requirements are university based, licensure based, or at the request and/or feedback of advisory boards and/or faculty.

Next, teacher candidates receive continued professional development throughout their program and intensified in the internship semester. Career Services is made available to our students to help them look for employment, and students further prepare by participating in mock interviews. Finally, the red light is always on at the station. Whether by visit (face-to-face or virtual), phone call, text, or email, all of our faculty and supervisors are in the house and ready to assist, even if it's as small as getting a cat out of the tree.

LOOKING TO THE FUTURE

As our programs continue to grow, it is exciting to think that we are growing our own mentors. Teacher candidates will have the opportunity to pay it forward once they have been teaching for three years. It is very exciting, because we will have even more contacts in the schools, and we know what they learned and experienced in their teacher preparation program.

One goal we have is to create a 911 support system. For our MAT students who are out teaching in the schools, they often need some more support especially because they can start teaching from their very first class in the program. Some private and charter schools do not require full licensure, so many of our teacher candidates work in these settings. Most of the time, these are very good settings. However, we have had a few that really struggled with a lack of curriculum, administrative support, and structure. In those instances, our candidates really need our help. Several have standing weekly appointments—tackling one problem at a time and being encouraged to keep going. However, we have many that could benefit from this service.

Ideally, our 911 system would work like a personal alert safety system device. It is our teacher candidate's safety system and distress signal. Just as firefighters have it clipped to their gear, our students will be armed with contact information to a 911-type support desk. It can be "manually triggered" by the student simply activating their personal alert safety system device and letting us know they're struggling and need help. Sometimes, however, teacher candidates do not know they are truly struggling or are too embarrassed to ask. In this instance, when they go "horizontal," the personal alert safety system device is "automatically triggered" by their mentor or administrator contacting us on their behalf.

Finally, it would be wonderful to track our MAT students from the first class to internship through the disposition rubric. How do their dispositions change? What improves? What was a strength that is now a weakness? Then, how can we help in those areas where we see a slide? What additional support structures could we put in place to eliminate the downhill slide proactively?

CLOSING THOUGHTS

It is easy to write off all problems as the intern's fault or the intern's problem. We can't just say it's their problem. If one vital component is missing such as the supervisor not providing timely feedback or a mentor going through a divorce and taking it out on intern, it breaks down the relationship and the process. Working with teacher candidates and scaffolding them has to be holistic. Often, we are quick to dismiss them or write them off. It's easier. It's quicker. It's less messy.

Too often in higher education, we lose sight of the fact that while these are adults (over the age of eighteen), they are still students. We forget how we treat students, how we accommodate students, how we modify for students. They have bad days. They have lives outside of the school. We do not know everything they're going through. Do they have adequate shelter? Are they having to work to put themselves through school? Is that work–school balance manageable? Do they have food? Do they have children? Are they taking care of ailing parents? The list goes on and on. There are so many social issues students of all ages confront. We cannot forget to meet them where they are. Let me say that again. We cannot forget to meet them where they are.

Teacher candidates need affirmation. Reassurance. Support. Empathy. Understanding. When struggling, the last thing they need to hear is, "Get it together or you're out of the program." Proactive structures need to be in place. Supports need to be made available, and when it comes to putting a teacher candidate under a contract, we need to remember this contract goes two ways. We have a side to uphold in helping the student remedy their deficiencies. Meet them where they are, and scaffold them to where they need to be. Some plants need just a little extra time to grow.

Can you be proactive? *Yes!* Should you be proactive? *Yes!* Does it take time? *Yes!* Does it take work? *Yes!* Is it worth it? *Absolutely!*

FIVE
Building Effective Partnerships and Relationships

When we consider quality, thriving relationships, several scenarios come to mind. We consider couples that make marriage beautiful and fruitful, friendships that bloom into sisterhoods and brotherhoods, parents and children who create life and are not just going through the motions. Likewise, we think of teachers, students, parents, administrators, and school support personnel combining forces to ensure that students succeed, realizing the infinite power of collaboration and community. Relationships that work are the foundation for partnerships that thrive, evolve, and impact. All the while, we hear Julie Andrews belting, "the hills are alive," as a montage of smiling faces and loving moments oscillate through our minds.

RELATIONSHIPS: THE FOUNDATION

Undoubtedly, relationships are fundamental when it comes to creating viable, lasting partnerships that stand the test of time. When relationships work, true synergy is possible, and everyone reaps the benefits. Consider the relationship of the master gardener and her creations. From careful plant selection and purposeful networking to securing materials, tools, and advice to tending the soil and nurturing the seeds, she is ardently invested and involved in the care and growth of her garden. Her care and attention is like that of a mother to her children: it is purposeful, it is meaningful, and it is powerful. Once her garden is cultivated, all who witness its beauty and experience its ethereal impact are inspired.

On the contrary, when relationships struggle, dysfunction rules. Anyone who has served time in education knows all too well the implications when relationships suffer. How many of us have witnessed partnership breakups and breakdowns due to a lack of trust, insignificant issues, or simple miscommunication? Instead of "the hills are alive," we are treated to Guns N' Roses' "Welcome to the Jungle," and in this version, there are no fun and games.

DYSFUNCTION: A BYPRODUCT OF SURFACE-LEVEL RELATIONSHIPS

Without solid relationships, partnerships may be possible, but they are not rooted, and without these firmly established relationships, partnerships will always be at risk. Lasting, grounded partnerships require not only buy-in but also a major, continuous investment by *all* players, and these players must all have authorship in the process to experience the real significance that growth fosters. From teacher to teacher, teacher to parent, teacher to student, teacher to administration, and school partners to institutions, when relationships are strained, students ultimately feel the impact. All students.

When do functional relationships become dysfunctional relationships, and why do we walk from the hills of glory to the jungles of chaos? How does the master gardener manage the weeds when they threaten to destroy her most beloved garden? Most relationships face major challenges; however, without that cultivated soil, our relationships may not have the ability to withstand the winds of change and dissension that often come in education.

For just a moment, let me go there. If you work anywhere near the field in kindergarten through twelfth-grade public schools, you will not only understand but also will resoundingly join us when we portray our struggles here. From the institution perspective, our students are not always welcome, and we will go on record here as saying, "We don't get it." Think about it.

Specifically, we have had schools and districts in our area actually ban interns for periods of time due to faculty changes, curriculum updates, and reconfigurations. Adding insult to injury, some schools do not want future teachers to attend back-to-school professional developments and meetings. Wake up, educators! Future teachers need to witness change. They need to feel the pressures that educators are feeling in real time. Future teachers need to experience curriculum concerns and revisions. Future teachers need to be a part of the conversations about transitions and reformations that will ultimately impact them.

Without a working knowledge of the real struggles schools and teachers face, we are limiting future teachers' experiences and ultimately creating organizational learning disabilities.

Let's face it. None of us will teach forever. Eventually, even the diehards will have to pass the podium and the chalk, and it comforts us greatly to think we have had a guiding hand in leading new teachers through the paths of the teaching labyrinth that they will all face. If our students and our schools are where we love and serve through the many struggles we have all endured, why would we leave our legacy to chance? Again, it makes no sense.

Sheltering interns or hiding our dirty laundry and the real messes of our school worlds is not only ridiculous, but it is reckless. We are denying these future teachers the experiences they need, considering they will one day be the mentor, the administrator, the counselor, and the ultimate decision maker. Eventually, we will all leave the classroom. When we support teacher education through these vital, interconnected relationships, we pave the way for our legacies to continue.

Recently, we had a school representative declare that his teachers no longer wished to mentor because it is too much trouble. His teachers were unaware of this. In fact, several teachers from his building reached out asking why the university was no longer sending interns. There is always the classic case of miscommunication, and let's be honest, the university is normally to blame, yet quick in our attempts, suiting and hosing up, to save the day.

As placement coordinators, we send hundreds of emails a semester, knowing that most will not be read, let alone answered. If emails are not answered, we take to the phones. Without a doubt, communication is vital when building and sustaining relationships that work. The following scenario is only one example of how miscommunication can stain an experience.

MISCOMMUNICATION BEGETS BAD EXPERIENCE

"Good afternoon, Ms. Principal. I hope you are doing well. This is Ms. Field Placement with the State Teachers College, and I am following up to the placement requests I have been sending (and re-sending) you. Are you all interested in hosting an intern next semester?" I inquire.

"What?" Ms. Principal is clearly, audibly shocked. "You sent me a request? I am looking through my emails, and I don't have anything from you."

I reply, "Yes, I know you have been super busy. Perhaps those emails are still somewhere in my Gmail," I lie. "I have a request for seventh-grade science with Ms. Teacher. We were hoping to send you a wonderful intern in the spring."

"That's fine. Send them," Ms. Principal says.

"Okay, I will put you guys down. Thank you so much!" I respond.

All may seem well in this scenario; however, an issue of this nature is a situation in the making because verbal agreements often result in miscommunication where well-meaning mentors do not get notified they have an intern coming until we send an email welcoming them to mentoring. This results in several emails, confusion, and, to be honest, hostility in some cases. One time, a mentor contacted us and asked us to stop assigning her interns. Apparently, her principal told her we were to blame for her getting interns as if we just indiscriminately place interns without any discussion or permission.

Occasionally, schools can be downright disgruntled, viewing our efforts to place teacher candidates as a nuisance. We have actually had a school agree to host interns, but when the interns showed up for their first day, they were told to leave. All dressed up, filled with excitement, and prepared, these interns had the doors of the school slammed in their faces. Because an administrator had forgotten they agreed to host, these interns were not only humiliated but were also terrified that this experience would tarnish their experience.

Even after we swooped in to save the day, fire hose and logical explanations in hand, we shouldered the blame for the miscommunication and clear lack of preparation and professionalism demonstrated by this administrator. Responsibility was accepted but not by the responsible party. Although the fire had been extinguished, another fire is imminent due to a failure to fix the faulty wiring in our relationship.

There is always the classic tale of a mentor who has had a bad experience and incites a war against all humanity, especially teacher education. Instead of working together through issues, we often create conundrums that only result in issues for our students—all students. It is as if educators forget that we have all been there. Our first semester on the job served as a true baptism by fire. One of our most seasoned, exceptionally talented mentors struggled with an intern who, admittedly, was a major source of concern—a true black swan.

Throughout his early field experiences, this guy had managed to receive glowing reviews with lessons that delighted his mentors, students, and supervisors; grades and testing scores that proved he knew his content; and a professional manner well beyond his years. He was at the top of his game, and we knew that placing him with an incredible, powerhouse mentor would be the apex of his already incredible experiences.

After Christmas break, right before his final internship experience, he arrived at our first orientation late, looking disheveled and disoriented. Instead of his clean, professional persona, he looked like he had been with the gardener, planting the morning away before he realized he had a meeting. He was a mess. Throughout the orientation, he was uneasy, and this guy who was once attentive and excited about teaching appeared to have been replaced by someone who looked like he had just left the filming of *Naked and Afraid* where he was a contestant. He was making everyone nervous.

After the meeting, he claimed that he overslept and would be ready for his internship that next Monday. Immediately and somewhat frantically, we reached out to his program coordinator and supervisor. We all had concerns and knew something was amiss; however, based on his record of success, other than a strange orientation episode, we were unable to ascertain a real understanding.

Once again, his first weeks at his internship were great; he was the shining star we knew he could be. We all reached out to his amazing mentor who said he was doing fine, and she had no concerns. Just as we were settling into what appeared to be a smooth semester, that pesky "black swan" entered. As a courtesy check, we called the mentor who had initially said that things were okay, but after several minutes into the conversation, we discovered things were anything but okay.

Not only had our intern been late most days, he was not performing well in the classroom. His once professional demeanor had transformed into a rebel without a cause.

This intern was not only confrontational with the mentor but had taken to attacking other teachers in the hallway. Not only was he defiant, but he also behaved bizarrely. The mentor claimed that she had prepared a hot cup of coffee for herself, placing her personal mug on her desk, and within minutes she noticed he had snatched it up and was enjoying every drop. Her desk had become his desk, and the students were the least of his concerns. He had initiated no teaching at all. Likewise, the mentor claimed that he was on his phone and drifting around the building most days, behaving bizarrely and erratically.

This was a 911 situation. Knowing that she liked to handle fires herself, we asked her to allow us to intervene, but she still held out hope she could manage this fire on her own, not wanting to create an awkward situation for him. Again, we pleaded for her to allow us to pull him in, and she countered that she would have never told us if she thought we would override her opportunity to work with him herself.

> Within weeks, however, things erupted into an apocalyptic fire, and we had no choice but to pull him from her classroom. Although she was initially upset, we knew we had a major problem on our hands, and time was not on our side. From that moment on, the mentor refused to work with another intern again, and her fury didn't stop there. Not only did she never mentor again, but also the school was now filled with a smoke that clouded our very partnership. Sadly, we never had a real relationship; therefore, the war waged against our institution had few allies on the inside. When we fail to address the cause, the root issue, and our relationships are not firmly established, we will eventually lose the relationship and the battle. Everything goes up in smoke!
>
> As pre-service teachers, we can all relate to entering a building for the first time, wanting nothing more than to find our place in the profession, seeking a relationship that will serve to guide us through the sometimes murky waters of the school business. Never did we consider that we were not wanted, that some schools actually would rather seal themselves off than open themselves up to innovations in teacher education. In reality, it seems as if we want to blame others for the woes in teacher education or miseducation. "It's their fault. The college is not preparing them. The schools are not preparing them. Their parents are not preparing them"; however, we must remember that *we are they*.
>
> No matter how much we may love the blame game and have mastered various levels of play, blame is a byproduct of dysfunction. Our inability to accept our responsibility to teacher education as a community of educators is a byproduct of dysfunction. Likewise, miscommunication and indifference are byproducts of dysfunction. Surface-level relationships that hinge on everything going perfectly are doomed to dysfunction eventually. Even the best of the best sometimes get it wrong. Inevitability, black swans find their way into our relationships. It is a fact, and our superficial relationships cannot withstand the shock of the sight.
>
> Knowing that relationships are going to face struggles is only part of the battle; it is in our working through those myriad struggles that together we will discover great relationships take work and an understanding of the big picture; in addition, having awareness of how these vital relationships can mutually benefit all students is just the beginning.

We Are They: Changing Our Thinking

Training our future educators is on all of us. Partnerships that hold this shared vision as they work together stand to benefit immensely. We are they. What we create together will ultimately serve our students, schools, and communities. If you do not think you play a part in this continuum, you are wrong. We are all members of this village, and as long as we are partaking, we are they.

Reframing our way of thinking here is a must. Most of us know all too well how university supervisors are viewed by the public schools. I have heard the term "ivory tower" mentioned on more than one occasion. When we step outside of the tower and into the villages and actually participate by serving, a transformation occurs. Not only do we reconnect and recollect, reflecting on our own calls to teach, but we also begin to see education from a perspective other than our own. Our investment and involvement will open doors and minds, creating a paradigm shift in schools where we serve.

Quality, thriving partnerships do not just magically happen, despite our incessant wishing. As a matter of fact, they are tremendous work—the product of constant keeping. The gardener's hands are always tending—they are always working.

CULTIVATING RELATIONSHIPS THAT WORK

For those partnerships that thrive, there is no magic formula. We wish there were. As a matter of fact, the commonalities are not shocking; on the contrary, they are quite simple. According to Maslow, our need for belonging and acceptance is only trumped by our need for food and shelter. Without a doubt, Maslow's hierarchy of needs is at the heart of what teachers do every day. Through love and acceptance, we establish and cultivate relationships that allow teaching and learning to occur. Belonging and acceptance form the foundation of trusting, respectful relationships that foster true collaboration and mutually beneficial partnerships.

RELATIONSHIPS THAT WORK: TRUTH IN HARMONY

In all of our work with school partners, we have found success. This success is built on establishing and cultivating relationships. In order to do so, we have found a word that encompasses the tenets of a strong relationship: *HARMONY*.

H—Honesty

Open communication is the source of honesty. Be honest about what you can and cannot do. What resources can you provide and what's off the table? Never overpromise, say what you mean, and mean what you say. Partnerships get in trouble when lies enter the agreement, and we have seen this firsthand.

We have been told repeatedly that good partnerships ebb and flow depending on the tide of change, but if we are honest with each other, changes that thwart good partnerships suggest superficiality. We have personally witnessed several changes in leadership since assuming our roles as field placement coordinators, and we are finding that in places where we have relationships, based on honesty and trust, we struggled less in transitions because we were established. We are not in the buildings, *taking*. On the contrary, we are in the buildings, *giving*.

Do our students benefit? You bet. Do our partnerships benefit? Immensely! Do we have struggles? Yes, and when we do, we do not seek to cover up mistakes. We own our faults. Perfection in field placement is not possible. Does honesty make us vulnerable? It does, but that is the beauty of the process. It is in our vulnerability that we grow together and discover new paths of innovation.

A—Authenticity

Within an honest framework of communication and functioning comes authenticity, and from authenticity comes value. Most of our high-quality fields are authentic. We are now terming them "organic" due to their development being from the source. Again, our fixation on the master gardener comes to play here. An organic field is grown from everyone's needs. We are not bringing a cookie-cutter class to the school and requesting certain cookie-cutter opportunities. When we approach a prospective partner about creating a field, we always ask about their needs and how we can help. From their needs, we examine how we can shape our courses and field to create organic opportunities. This authenticity can only come from actually working with the schools. You have to be a part of the community for the organic field to grow.

For example, the reading courses featured in the proactive chapter are organic fields, grown from the needs of both our partners and the university. When approaching the school about hosting the undergraduate course on their campus (less than a mile from our campus), we asked about their needs and concerns. Before the meeting's conclusion, it was revealed that not only did they need reading assistance for their students, but they needed some English as a Second or Other Language (ESOL) interventions as well. Throughout the school year, the author hosted ESOL classes where her students were able to come and learn all about ESOL strategies, guided by her instruction and assistance. This was a rare opportunity for her students, and the target ESOL group benefited from our "Let's Get Cooking" Friday classes. This was never on her radar, but, together with her school partners, she made this field purposeful and authentic.

R — Responsibility

University people, you do not put the *part* in partnership. Collectively, we must work together with schools. They are not designed to serve us. You do not get to call the shots. As a matter of fact, having just recently come from the classroom to the university, we can promise you this: You are not always relevant nor are you always welcome due to some of your attitudes. Leave them at the door and come with a willingness to work with public schools, not for and not against.

We have a responsibility to serve one another, working in tandem to serve *all students*. We must take responsibility for our actions and understand when we blaze through public schools, we are responsible to not only the university but to the schools. As school people, we think we have established the importance of why we must share the load of teacher education, and we understand that working with university people is not always easy; however, we have a responsibility to one another. We have a responsibility to educate *all students*.

M — Meaningful

Are we not all on a journey of meaning? At the heart of our very existence is meaning and purpose. When we are in a trusting relationship, we seek a collective meaning. How can this relationship become even more meaningful and have a lasting impact?

Considering the gardener and her horticultural creations, her meaning is evident in the beauty of her masterpieces. Beauty stems from the relationship she has nurtured. This is not something that we alone can make, but in tandem with partners, we create meaning together, exploring how to create meaning for all students and faculty involved in our partnerships. Where we experience the most synergy, we have meaningful relationships where we all experience authorship and significance. We make time for meaning and, above all, ensure meaning is at the center of our shared vision and mission. Reaching out to partners and co-constructing meaningful field experience is paramount.

Last semester, a student wrote one of the most impactful letters to one of the authors. In his note, he thanked her for guiding him and inspiring him in such a meaningful experience while working at our reading field site. He shared with the author how this field had provided him with strategies, forcing him to rethink differentiation and prepared him to address literacy in his content area classes. Closing the letter, he stated, "Your guidance and encouragement throughout the field experience reaffirmed my decision to teach. You have had an impact." Meaningful and impactful — we cannot imagine two more powerful words to associate with high-quality, authentic field experience.

O—Open-minded

Some of the very best partnerships we have are due in large part to the diversity of ideas that have blossomed from the shared vision. We all have our thoughts of how partnerships and field opportunities should look, but our thoughts may not always work within real-world settings. Having an open mind and a willingness to take risks with our partners injects the relationship with vulnerability that is invigorating to a partnership.

An example of this: One of the authors, along with an incredible team at her university, began working with a residential foster home facility throughout the year, providing after-school tutoring and assistance. Our students and even faculty worked to ensure our students in the field are seeing us active, working side by side with them to assist kindergarten through twelfth-grade students. We saw tremendous gains throughout the year, but the summer proved to be problematic. Without access to learning opportunities, students were falling behind.

Working together with the foster facility and the school administration, we were able to provide a summer camp to promote summer literacy. After the educational specialist for the group expressed real concerns about their summer learning during one of our many meetings, we brainstormed and discussed ways, by working together, we could make a true difference. From this partnership, we have grown a successful, mutually beneficial field placement. Again, this required an open mind on all parties' behalves. We cannot enter agreements looking out for our own interests. By having open minds, we see where real needs are and can work collectively, creating innovative field opportunities.

Partnerships sometimes need a spark, and by having open mind, we recognize the importance of evaluating ourselves. Just as relationships and gardens need constant tending and nurturing, so do our partnerships. At some point, we have to look at our partnerships as we would our most prized relationship and say, "Is this really working? Have I created a garden or a neglected, weedy mess?" Constantly assess partnerships and their effectiveness.

One way to check the pulse of a field placement is to survey. From students and mentors to our administrators, we send surveys every semester, gauging our progress. Currently, we use Qualtrics and Google Forms to generate our responses, and we actually use the information we glean from these surveys. Many decisions have been made regarding times and dates of field offerings, including adding and removing sites, depending on feedback from our participants.

N—No "I" in Team

We are all in this together. Just think *High School Musical*, and you get the picture. We are they, and until we truly get this concept, our students will ultimately fail to reap the benefits of what authentic field can present. By investing ourselves, like the master gardener, in the students we teach and the schools in which they practice, we not only view the beauty, we create it.

We should be *present*. Physically, mentally, and emotionally, we bring ourselves to the schools and serve the schools, knowing that our continuous investment is making a difference, not just for the university and our partners, but also for our community. We are a team, and we support each other. We are not alone in venturing out to serve school campuses throughout our area; likewise, public school partners come to the university and actually help train our interns. In true partnership fashion, they bring their expertise and their service to us. Believe it or not, they actually have street cred, and our interns greatly appreciate the insight our partner administrators and teachers bring to the conversation.

When we approach field placement with the best interests of *all students* in mind, we begin to see where public schools may struggle to meet the university's demands. When public schools and community organizations see that we are working alongside them, not ahead of them, we begin to enjoy the benefits of a team approach.

Our focus must be team oriented, and our vision must be shared.

Y—Yield

We are servants first. At the very epicenter of education are service-minded educators. These servants do not have to be seen or rewarded for their service; they yield to the demands of education, seeking constantly to improve and reform. Where servants convene and serve, harvests of great abundance are possible. Accepting our calls to service require us to yield to the demands and the messiness of organic field opportunities. Yielding to the service is the ultimate reward, experiencing successes; one student at a time, and the fruit of the labor is authentic learning where content learning and practice converge. Every day we serve in the field is a day we get to witness why we accepted the call to teach—to be a game changer.

Yes, we do acknowledge that throughout the jungle, venomous snakes slither and poisonous spiders lurk; however, within the core, pure intentions and servants do still exist and serve, creating and crafting a shared vision with partners based on meaning and purpose of all involved, not just one side, and yielding to this vision with service, not because of obligation but because we make promises and keep them. If you say you are going to assist the school, then do it. No excuses. When we see and embrace the big picture, we can then understand the rationale behind the movements we make in partnerships, and we must always remember that we are servants first.

BE A VISIONARY

We have all heard of the incredible power of visualization, and when building partnerships and new, innovative field experiences, visualization is fuel to creation and implementation. Want to reach a desired goal with field? Paint yourself in the gallery of your goals. Would the master gardener just haphazardly throw seeds of every variety into soil without making plans and preparations? One master gardener actually sketches her creations and researches the different plants, their growth patterns, heat tolerance, in addition to many other criteria, before ever planting a single seed. This master sees the garden of the future in the soil of today. Thinking outside the box is so important when it comes to visionary practices, but most importantly, we must visualize collectively, creating a shared vision with our partners, constructing visually an organic, community garden.

How is shared vision possible with so many players who have so many diverse interests and needs? Everyone must see the value in sharing the vision and the load. This is not something we can simply communicate; it really must be experienced or witnessed, and we have to promote our successful programs, documenting our progress. For example, one of our sites has experienced an incredible year with many of our school site students experiencing substantial growth. As a matter of fact, one student's reading level increased by three grade levels, putting her at grade-level reading. Although we could attribute one student's growth to many other variables, every student in our program experienced significant gains. Not only have we shared this with our colleagues, but also the school administration is sharing this information with other administrators throughout the district. Word is getting out that we are crafting opportunities that truly benefit all students, and others are now wanting in on the action.

Communicate with one another, each sharing visions and dreaming big. One theme that resonates throughout this chapter is the importance of communication; when crafting a vision, open, honest communication cannot be overlooked. We are reaching out now to our partners, constructing plans for the following years. We reflect on what did not work while celebrating what did. When we fail to reflect with our partners, creating a shared vision is almost impossible. Communication, in good times and bad, is vital. We do not want the only experiences we have with our partners to be when we are showing up suited up for a fire. On the contrary, we seek to share in the good times as well. When we share in the joys of authentic experiences, it establishes connections that form the foundation of partnerships. Instead of fighting alone, we are joined by a team of invested educators. Instead of fighting a blazing inferno of a fire, we are throwing water and dirt on some embers.

No shared vision can come to fruition without a willingness to see it through. We have to be willing to work, and when we say work, we mean work *hard*. Not only do we set up field sites for our interns, but also we serve at several sites. We tutor. We teach. We intervene. We model. Side by side with interns and site mentors, we work together. Having a strategy to give life to the vision is great, but without a willingness to work, strategies are worthless.

Plans mean nothing without implementation. Once you have a shared vision, give it life, and everyone must play a part. We serve at our sites, but we are not alone. Our partners serve with us. We are all working to ensure our students are getting the very best experience possible. From our vision, a plan is devised, and from our plan, roles are determined. We all have jobs, and everyone is invested.

In conclusion, we all have to check ourselves and leave our attitudes at the door. Oftentimes, when we hear of the amazing fields—those Blue Ribbon field programs—we just want to walk away and pretend they don't exist. Creating field opportunities for our students can be grueling and time consuming. Not every field site secretary is kind. Sometimes, teachers can feel threatened by our presence. Occasionally, our own students complain about having to drive to the field site. Sadly, not all kindergarten through twelfth-grade students are excited about our presence. There are aspects we cannot control; however, there are many, systematically, that we must.

No matter what we face in the field, we will remain calm and positive, checking our own attitude and remembering it is always about the students we teach and the ones we reach. It is impossible to create visionary field opportunities when we are stuck in routines of familiarity and isolation. Creating partnerships based on thriving relationships is fundamental to designing and implementing organic, meaningful field opportunities. Together, we can do this.

SIX
Where Do You Go Next?

Where do we go next? We go with the flow. Superheroes arrive in the nick of time to save the day, but they seldom anticipate and prevent the threat. What is heroic about that? We live in a world that is ever changing and unpredictable. The attitudes and values of our teacher candidates change from year to year, and we must adapt to these changes and solve the problems that result. We must be the superheroes that fly in to eliminate the threat to quality education and quality educators for the students who come into classrooms every day expecting the best our teachers can give them.

KEEPING IT FRESH

The great thing about teacher candidates is their fresh perspective and enthusiasm. It bubbles out of most of them. They are so excited about getting into the classrooms, working with students, and making a difference. What they do not realize is that these are the traits that make them superheroes. They bring an energy into the school that can revitalize and invigorate a tired teacher. They can give new hope to students in classrooms who have fallen into a rut or been labeled as a problem.

Teacher candidates do not realize any of these things. They only know that they are finally in a classroom, and they are eager to learn and to help. Teachers who have worked with teacher candidates know about the energy and excitement they can bring into a classroom. That is why they continue to accept our candidates. The energy they bring is a great marketing tool that we can use as we search for more school partners. They need our candidates. They need their enthusiasm, ideas, and creative spirit. Partner schools have an opportunity to get help from an enthusiastic teacher candidate and have an opportunity to watch them in action for an entire semester.

VALUING THE INTERNSHIP EXPERIENCE

We must make sure our teacher candidates who are placed as student teachers understand that their time in the schools is like a long job interview. If they make the most of it, they could have a great opportunity to continue working in the school with pay!

Many of our Master of Arts in Teaching candidates are teachers of record in their own classrooms. We supply support and resources as needed for them. We encourage them to build a network of support both within their school community and with our university. Many times we hear from these students who were in our classes. They ask for materials and ideas that we shared with them in class as they see the relevance of the material in their classes.

PROBLEMS WILL ARISE

Pet peeves are like the pests in the plants of a master gardener's garden. They are ever multiplying, and, when you control or dispose of one, another will come to take its place. Like the master gardener, we must keep a watchful eye on the problem, anticipate and head off what we can, prune the branches that will never produce, and fertilize what is left to give strength, endurance, and support.

Like a talented and observant gardener, we will use what we learn from previous experiences to anticipate problems and prepare our programs to address deficiencies our candidates might have and educate them on dispositions they will need in order to be successful. Like every good gardener, we will not assume that our candidates will have the resources or social knowledge they need, and we will be sure to include those tools in our programs.

Rules may not be followed. Behavior may not always be socially acceptable. Mentors and candidates will not always behave in an ethical, professional manner, and communication will not always be adequate for the needs of all concerned, *but* it will be better and will continue to improve through the efforts of dedicated professionals who commit themselves to the improvement of education for students through improving the education of teacher candidates.

Professionalism is not just another term used in education. It is a way of life for good educators. We need to educate our teacher candidates about the meaning of professionalism and its importance in the profession. We need to remind them of their experiences with teachers and how it felt to work with a dedicated professional versus how it felt to work for someone who was not committed to the education of their students. Feelings are powerful motivators. Just as a parent cautions a child that fire is hot in order to save them from getting burnt, we must caution our candidates about the importance of being professionals before they and their students get burned.

We must help teacher candidates to understand the importance of preparation, empathy, and trust. If candidates are prepared for their lessons, they can adapt to whatever conditions might occur during the act of teaching. If candidates demonstrate empathy for students and their skills and roadblocks, then students will learn to trust them and take a chance on communicating and making mistakes.

DISPOSITIONAL CONCERNS

Disposition issues will continue to appear just as fires continue to occur for firefighters. If a fireman takes responsibility for the fire he fights, will that impact the possibility of it happening again? As we continue to fight the fires of disposition issues, we also need to learn to allow teacher candidates to accept the consequences of their actions and learn from them. They can't learn from their mistakes if we never allow them to happen, or if we follow them with an extinguisher to put out the fires they cause. We have to create a system for them to own their mistakes, identify what they did to cause them, and make a plan for addressing them so it does not happen again. If we follow this philosophy, we also must support the educators who mentor our candidates. We must make sure the lines of communication stay open and our responses to issues are prompt, relevant, and effective.

Many times, disposition issues follow a pattern. We look for these patterns and incorporate what we see into information we share at our orientation sessions, workshops we offer for teacher candidates, and in our classrooms. We share these patterns with colleagues in our departmental meetings to increase awareness so they can help us to address the issues in their classes, and we have used this information to include a session in our orientation that specifically addressed dispositions.

DIFFERENT, VARIED, AND VALUED PERSPECTIVES

Different perspectives are a way of life on a college campus. These campuses offer perspectives on education that you will find nowhere else. Like Data on *Star Trek*, we need to recognize that we are removed from K–12 public education, and the only way we can remain a relevant part of the educational process is to seek out the perspectives of practitioners in the field, search for ways to provide them with what they need to be more effective and efficient, and show up by working alongside our students in authentic field experiences.

We also need to respect the perspective that each involved party brings to the table in field placements. Professors bring their knowledge of research and publishing to the table. They can identify trends and gaps. Clinical instructors from higher education bring their personal experience in the field and the connections they formed while working in public schools. Supervising mentor teachers bring their knowledge of the students and the school. They are experts with the curriculum, the schedule, and their students. Teacher candidates bring the enthusiasm and perspective of fresh eyes on our classrooms and our techniques and a different view of relationships between teachers and students.

THE IMPORTANCE OF PARTNERSHIPS AND RELATIONSHIPS

For this reason, partnerships and relationships are essential. Like Batman and Robin, we are more powerful and more effective as a team. If it takes a village to raise a child, then we must not just be a part of the village, we must be an essential part. If school teachers and administrators act in loco parentis, then we need to assume the role of the grandparents who serve as resources and support for the teachers and administrators in the schools.

MAINTAINING PROACTIVITY

In order to be relevant, we must be proactive. We must keep up with state mandates and regulations and make sure our teacher candidates are prepared to meet them. We must establish a good network of communication with the state department of education and participate in trainings and staff development they offer public schools.

We should also communicate with schools to let them know we are available to help them train their teachers in the latest programs and best practices by offering our services for staff development. We must let them know that we have resources to help them and their teachers. When we are available to the schools to help in this way, we are forming the relationships we need to have in order to be part of the cycle of learning that the students need.

In this effort, we offer some of our field courses at local public school campuses. Our students are assigned to work with students at local schools in the morning. In the afternoon, they meet for class in a local middle school where they share their experiences and learn about best practices.

WOES IN A NONTRADITIONAL PROGRAM

Nontraditional programs provide the unique opportunity of teacher candidates actually working as the teacher of record in classrooms. This makes it especially important to establish good lines of communication between the university supervisor, teacher candidate, and mentor teacher. Teacher candidates who are teachers of record need all of the support we can give. Many times, they do not feel comfortable asking for assistance because they feel we will think they cannot handle the job.

Sometimes they are so overwhelmed they do not know what kind of assistance they should request. They need help with everything. Often, especially in large urban schools, they receive assignments that more experienced and knowledgeable teachers do not want. These are some of the toughest assignments.

One of our teacher candidates was hired in an urban school to teach a kindergarten class. Three weeks after the school year began, she was transferred to a second-grade classroom. The classroom was out of control. A more experienced teacher had been responsible for the class but used her seniority to transfer back to kindergarten, leaving the teacher candidate to teach the troubled second-grade class. Some of the problems she encountered included students who got up to go to other students' desks during instruction, students who refused to follow any directions that the candidate gave, students who could not leave the classroom alone or they would run away, as well as a student who was very aggressive and who finally beat up another student in the classroom.

Our teacher candidate got very little support from the administration in the school. Two other teachers on her hall helped her as much as they could. We worked with this candidate to find resources that would help her to gain control of her class. The teacher candidate formed a partnership with a teacher in our psychology department who helped her with ideas and strategies to help her students with their behavior. By the end of the semester, she had achieved miraculous things in her classroom. This is only one example of the unique problems encountered by teacher candidates in our nontraditional program and the resources and assistance that universities can provide for them.

Strong partnerships are developed over time and only last if they are nurtured. We will continue to nurture our partnerships as a master gardener nurtures her garden. New partnerships strengthen our program and expand our resources. We will continue to search for new partners and find ways to strengthen these partnerships by offering partner schools resources that we have available.

COMMUNICATION 101—ESSENTIAL FOR SUCCESS

Communication is essential for any program to grow and improve. Through experience with what is working and what is not working, we will continue to improve our methods of communication with teacher candidates, supervising mentors, and partner schools.

Communication is a part of each of our field programs. We communicate with schools through our teacher candidates, through email and messaging, through phone conversations, and in person. We communicate with any method that our partner school prefers. This communication pays off with renewed partnerships, reduced frustration, and a better experience for our teacher candidates.

THE POWER OF LOOKING

Finally, remember the Dick and Jane books that were the first primers for many older adults? The first word they learned, the biggest word of all was "look." We must look at our field programs. We must look at what is working and make it grow. We must look at what is holding us back and eliminate it or improve it. We must look at programs offered by other universities, and we must attend conferences to meet colleagues and share ideas and information.

Furthermore, we must look at educational trends and make certain we are staying up to date and relevant. In other words, we must follow Kolb's Learning Cycle research:

1. Plan
2. Do
3. Reflect
4. Conclude

The reflecting and concluding steps can serve as a basis for correctly planning our next steps. It serves as a base for modifying the "overall plan" for field experiences.

We must remember that we are preparing our teacher candidates for a global classroom. We cannot limit them or their potential.

SEVEN

Professional Development and Resources

Professional development is a vital part of the teaching profession. It is the way educators stay current on issues, abreast of the latest instructional tools and strategies, and obtain needed information in areas needing improvement or to be further developed. Because we realize the importance of professional development to in-service teachers, our pre-service teacher programs have infused these opportunities throughout each and every semester.

PROFESSIONAL DEVELOPMENT: MIDDLE-LEVEL PROGRAM

In our middle-level programs, students can become members of the Collegiate Middle Level Association. Students are invited annually to a conference that is held at the university, and local teachers, administrators, and faculty are invited to submit proposals for presentations on important topics in middle-level education. Our department chair graciously pays for fifty students to attend at no charge. Others may attend for a small fee that covers the cost of breakfast and lunch. Area teachers and administrators also attend as the professional development is generally on timely topics such as the Teacher Excellence and Support System (TESS), classroom management, dyslexia, and diversity, to name a few.

PROFESSIONAL DEVELOPMENT: INTERNSHIP

During internship, professional development is a vital time for us as internship coordinators. We have the students on campus so that we can address any questions or concerns, allow them an opportunity to collaborate with their peers, and provide them some invaluable professional development geared toward helping them find their first job and transitioning through a successful first year of teaching.

Two professional development days are offered each semester. The first one provides a refresher of TESS, which is very important as final assignments are completed and is critical when interviewing for teaching positions as this is the teacher evaluation system in our state. A snippet of school law is reviewed, and then we invite in administrators. Topics covered include integrating technology in the schools, documenting TESS through artifacts, and exhibiting professionalism in schools. Our administrators are school partners who host numerous interns in their buildings each semester, hire recent graduates, and are well-versed in their subject areas.

Also during the first professional development day, university faculty speak to our candidates regarding our key programs and assessments, ensuring the assignments and needed technology are understood, and our science, technology, engineering, and mathematics resource center director reminds our students of all of the free materials available for check-out to interns and area teachers.

Finally, a real need had been recognized in our students in understanding how to work with children coming from impoverished homes. Many of our students grew up and went to school in smaller districts, some rural, where there may not have been a lot of diversity and/or exposure to impoverished families. When placed in more diverse or urban settings, our students are struggling. Therefore, from our observations as well as feedback from school administrators and human resource officers, we have worked to meet this need. Three faculty were sent to Ruby Payne training, and now these faculty integrate their knowledge into their coursework, internship professional development, and other professional development on campus and throughout area districts.

For the second professional development day, our students start the day with mock interviews. We invite superintendents, principals, and human resource officers to come to campus to hold mock interviews for our interns and give them feedback on how to improve when interviewing for the positions they hope to obtain. Interestingly, these officials are sometimes looking to fill immediate needs, and some of our students have received job offers. After visiting with one of the local charter schools, one of our candidates went through the complete interview process at that school and was offered a job teaching physical education.

After the mock interviews, the administrators and human resource officers hold a panel discussion where they share pros and cons of the interviews in the spirit of continuous improvement. Questions are also fielded directly from the candidates regarding resumes, dress, and interview tips. One of our area administrators offers to proofread each and every resume if sent to her, and she holds true to that promise! This is followed up with the university's career services department also giving interview and professional dress tips and fielding any other questions the candidates may have.

Next, one of the highlights of the day occurs. A diverse panel of teachers and faculty covering English language learners, special education, and dyslexia respond to questions the candidates have. This has proven to be a real eye-opener for many of our candidates. There is so much information, so much to know, as a first-year teacher regarding accommodations, modifications, differentiation, and diverse learners.

Finally, a local principal comes and speaks regarding the importance of building relationships with children and making those connections especially in order to be successful in the urban classroom. As Rita Pierson so eloquently stated, "Teaching and learning should bring joy. How powerful would our world be if we had kids who were not afraid to take risks, who were not afraid to think, and who had a champion? Every child deserves a champion, an adult who will never give up on them, who understands the power of connection, and insists that they become the best that they can possibly be" (Rita Pearson, "Every Kid Needs a Champion," *TED Talk*, 2013). Our students leave invigorated, motivated, eager, and ready to meet their students where they are, to start building those relationships, and always to maintain dignity when disciplining.

PROFESSIONAL DEVELOPMENT: CANDIDATES ON A PROVISIONAL LICENSE

In our Master of Arts in Teaching (MAT) program, candidates obtain jobs at various times throughout the year. Some are hired as late as October, and then in December and January, the cycle starts again. To help meet the needs of these candidates who start their jobs later in the year and miss the beginning of the year professional development, set-up, and establishing norms and rules, our program decided to host a S'mores Student Success day. Candidates on a provisional license or working in a private or charter school received priority registration and then additional seats were opened for candidates just interested in an additional day of learning.

Based on feedback from our candidates and the administrators who were hiring them, the day included strategies for classroom management, literacy strategies, changes to the dyslexia law, strategies for working with children with dyslexia, assessment strategies, and building a community of learners while establishing relationships with students. The professional development was well received and will become an annual event.

PROFESSIONAL DEVELOPMENT: YEARLY MASTER OF ARTS IN TEACHING SYMPOSIUMS

Due to high attrition rates, especially in urban school settings, an annual symposium was established for students in our MAT program. The symposium was designed to increase student success by addressing challenges that teachers, and most importantly, our candidates as teachers encounter. Administrators, faculty, and teachers from across the state presented various sessions.

During the first year of the symposium, the focus was on working in urban, rural, and suburban settings—particularly how different strategies might be more effective in different environments and classroom management. In the second year, the focus was on dyslexia, differentiation, and diversity.

PROFESSIONAL DEVELOPMENT: TECHNOLOGY

Technology is also a critical component in today's classroom. Because of this, we have invited presenters from Code.Org to teach our students how to code and provide them with the materials to teach their students to code. Having an Apple Distinguished Educator on the faculty doesn't hurt either, and he has helped create EdCamp and various other technology opportunities for our faculty and students.

PROFESSIONAL DEVELOPMENT: STUDENTS PRESENTING

It is very exciting when our students want to share about exciting things they are doing in the field. This past year, three of our MAT candidates presented at the Arkansas Literacy Association's fall conference regarding their work in the University of Central Arkansas' Reading Success Center as part of the course MAT 6314: Reading Difficulties. These students shared lessons learned, what they immediately took back with them to the classroom, how the experience shaped them as a teacher, and how the experience changed them. One of these students has gone on to be a literacy interventionist at one of our partner school districts.

ADDITIONAL RESOURCES

Professional development is not always enough, and sometimes we have to call upon additional resources.

For Praxis I Core exams, students in the undergraduate program receive free NorthStar access in their first teaching class. MAT students struggling with this exam as an admission requirement can also obtain free access.

While in internship, sometimes students need the opportunity for additional observations. While not enough improvement may have been shown before the first two, often adding one additional observation gives the candidate the chance to show their ongoing work. At times, additional faculty can even go out and conduct these observations, providing another set of eyes and ears for a struggling intern.

When possible, professional texts are provided for the students. At the last Students of Success Symposium, students received Sally Shaywitz's *Overcoming Dyslexia* and Ruby Payne's *A Framework for Understanding Poverty*. In previous years, students received Harry Wong's *Classroom Management* book. Additional copies are kept in our offices, so when students are struggling, we can provide some invaluable resources.

Finally, we assist our students in obtaining jobs by participating in the University of Central Arkansas' university-wide teacher fair as well as hosting several mini-fairs throughout the summer and early fall for those last-minute positions that need to be filled. This helps our students who are still trying to get jobs and our partners fill those positions with quality teachers.

LOOKING TO THE FUTURE

Each of our programs holds advisory group meetings every year and invites various constituents to include human resource officers, administrators, mentor teachers, current students, faculty, and alumni. During this time, data is shared from the previous year as well as what our faculty has determined as areas of strengths and weakness. Furthermore, ideas for improvement are shared, and we ask for our stakeholders to provide us with input.

From our most recent advisory group, we hear that more professional development is needed in Individual Education Plans, 504s, and accommodations and modifications when working with special populations. As always, our students can never get enough classroom management, and they would like continued guidance, support, and practice with working with parents. Interestingly, they are also asking for more field, which we are so graciously working to provide for them. Our students love the opportunities that are afforded to them, learn so much from them, and are anxious to learn even more before they're ready to embark upon their own classrooms.

Closing Thoughts

It has been a joy and an honor to write this book. Even colleagues working closely together do not truly know the depths of the passion, experience, and desire to make things better for education until embarking upon a project like this one. We learned we all have big jobs—different from one another—but bigger than any of us realized. We have come to appreciate each other's knowledge, expertise, and skills on a whole other level.

AMY'S FINAL THOUGHTS

> Tell me and I forget. Teach me and I remember. Involve me and I learn.
> —Benjamin Franklin

Field experience is where the rubber meets the road. I remember being in my teacher preparation program. I enjoyed the coursework, but I loved the field. The first time I ever went out was to Jefferson Elementary in the Little Rock School District. Mainly observing, I did have the opportunity to work with some children. It was exhilarating. Flash forward to a field experience in physical education at Julia Lee Moore, and I moved from observing to interacting with the children—leading parachute games!

But then came student teaching. The first time I stepped in front of Ms. Hawkins' fifth-grade class and taught a science lesson, I. Was. Hooked. I knew right then and there that teaching was my calling. I knew I wanted to do that again and again and again, because the feeling of teaching something, interacting with the children, engaging them in hands-on learning, and seeing the light bulb go off as new concepts clicked—I couldn't imagine anything better in the world.

And I was right—for fourteen years. Then came the opportunity to work on the other side of the table, and I am reinvigorated again. I'm still a teacher. I'm interacting with much older students, but I'm engaging them in hands-on learning, seeing the light bulb as new concepts click, and getting them fired up about teaching children to read. I am teaching teachers to not be the ones Dick Allington has described: Teachers who thought that fair instruction meant equality—giving to all students regardless of their needs. I want them to be the other teachers Dick Allington described: Teachers who understand that fair means equity—evening out differences between students; giving students what they need when they need it; meeting them where they are; leveling the playing field. Again, I have that feeling. I can't imagine anything better in the world.

Field experience is just hands-on learning for our pre-service teachers. I love seeing their excitement and remembering my joy when first interacting with children and a classroom and realizing this is who I am. I even more love seeing them realize this is who they are and witnessing the igniting of the passion.

While we have to be realistic and think about the attitudes we encounter, the big personalities, and the students that are just not meant to be teachers, we cannot become jaded and lost in the beautiful experiences we are a part of. I see some amazing teachers go out into the schools each and every day—excited and eager to meet their students where they are, know that all students can learn, and willing to be true advocates for children and positive change in education.

Those are the final thoughts I want to leave you with. We've spent an entire book preparing you for the others—relish in the ones that were born to be teachers, that make you proud, that make you get out of bed every morning on the hunt for the next teacher like that, that inspires you to be better.

CRYSTAL'S FINAL THOUGHTS

> Education is not the filling of a bucket, but the lighting of a fire.
> —William Butler Yeats

It is in the conclusion that we rediscover our beginnings. Writing this book, for me, has been a process in reflexivity where each experience sparked reflection—call it my own progress monitoring. Although this book is based on the experiences of educators and not the product of years of research, it holds valid truths given the rich nature of our lived experiences.

Like many of you, I have attended numerous professional developments, taken a multitude of teaching courses, and have read a surplus of books and studies about teaching, but being a teacher, being immersed in the culture of teaching, reaffirmed my love for this profession and the professionals we call teachers. With that love and understanding comes the harsh reality that not everyone can teach. We all know them and ask the same question, "How did they ever become teachers?" If anything, we hope this book has provided you with some thoughts on how to begin conversations and, likewise, begin the process of insisting on high-quality teacher education.

Developing strong partnerships with schools, mentors, and supervisors is vital when it comes to harnessing the experiences and the insight all of these players possess. Forming collaborative partnerships and creating a forum for open, honest dialogue can have an enormous impact on our teacher candidates. We can no longer afford to send ill-equipped teachers into the diverse, challenging field of teaching; however, this is not a problem for teacher education programs alone. It is a problem that we must collectively address.

No matter how much I think I may know about teaching, I am always reminded that my colleagues bring such rich experiences and insights to collaborations, and the same principle holds true when it comes to working with our partners. We really can learn from one another. Open your minds and let the real learning begin.

CHRIS' FINAL THOUGHTS

> Coming together is a beginning; keeping together is progress; working together is success.
> —Henry Ford

Field experience courses are a marriage between institutions of higher learning and public schools. As in all relationships, there is an initial meeting, a courtship, and eventually a proposal. When the partnership is confirmed, the marriage begins. Strengths and weaknesses on both sides are discovered and, if there is respect and commitment, strengths are built upon and weaknesses are examined and worked on until we make them strengths. The partnership only lasts if we work together to find solutions to the problems that teacher candidates present. Just as children bring new problems into a marriage, candidates bring issues into the classroom and the relationships with schools.

If we are lucky, candidates bring commitment, talent, and a caring attitude. If we are not so lucky, they bring problems and attitudes that test us and the partnership we have formed. What helps us to get through the problems is the commitment of all of us to what is best for the children we serve.

Coming together to write this book was an enlightening and rewarding venture. I say that not because we never work together, but because we had an opportunity to share and reflect on a much more detailed level. I come away from this experience with an enormous amount of respect for my colleagues and their commitment to improving field experiences for our students and, by doing so, improve the quality of education that students in public and private schools receive. As with all educators in the United States, they are overworked and underpaid, but they commit their talents, time, and resources every day as if they were being paid exorbitantly. Their dedication is impressive, and they are making a difference.

> Never doubt that a small group of thoughtful, committed people can change the world. Indeed, it is the only thing that ever has.
> —Margaret Meade

Closing Thoughts

We hope you, our readers, have found at least a nugget of information that is useful to you that you might implement in your programs. We would also love to hear from you and hear your ideas. We are all in this together. It is all of our jobs to ensure the best and brightest are filling our classrooms—giving our children the best chance possible.

> Education is not filling of a pail but the lighting of a fire.
> —William Butler Yeats

Appendix A
Master of Arts in Teaching
New Student Orientation

Time	Topic	Speaker
8:00 A.M.–8:05 A.M.	Welcome from program coordinator/department chair	
8:05 A.M.–9:05 A.M.	Introduction to the MAT program, PRAXIS, and licensure	
9:05 A.M.–9:35 A.M.	Academic integrity/plagiarism; what it means to be a graduate student	
9:35 A.M.–10:05 A.M.	MAT dispositions; time expectations	
10:05 A.M.–10:15 A.M.	Break	
10:15 A.M.–10:45 A.M.	Arkansas IDEAS	
10:45 A.M.–11:00 A.M.	Chalk and wire; TLC resources	
11:00 A.M.–12:00 P.M.	Lunch (on your own)	
12:00 P.M.–12:30 P.M.	Torreyson Library resources; APA manual	
12:30 P.M.–1:30 P.M.	MAT student panel	
1:30 P.M.–1:50 P.M.	Field experiences/professionalism	
1:50 P.M.–2:00 P.M.	Q & A; closing	
2:00 P.M.–3:00 P.M.	Sub-agencies	

Appendix B
Professional Growth Plan

PART I: PLAN
PART II: SUBMISSION
(This plan is to be submitted to your instructor no later than 5:00 P.M. on the day following our meeting.)

PLAN: Use the table below to develop a professional growth plan targeting a specific improvement goal for *each* component that was scored with a "1" unsatisfactory score.

NOTE: This cannot be done with one or two sentences. Your responses will indicate your understanding and commitment to addressing these issues. Minimal or general responses will be reflected on your grade for the class.

TESS Domain and Component (e.g., Domain 1C – Instructional Outcomes.)	List details with unsatisfactory scores. (e.g., Outcomes lack rigor. Outcomes are not suitable for many students in the class.)	Describe what you did that led to this score. (The teacher observing you and scoring your lesson should have shared the reasons behind the scores with you.)	Describe what you plan to do to address and improve this area of your teaching. (You must provide this response. Based on what you learned from your observing teacher, what do you need to do to improve?)	List resources you plan to use to achieve success. (Internet, print, and/or human resources.)

Appendix C
Internship Contract

Name:

ID #:

Course Deficits/Problem(s):

_____
_____
_____
_____
_____
_____

Praxis Deficits/Problem(s):

_____
_____
_____
_____
_____
_____

I will successfully complete the above listed Praxis requirement(s) by the completion of Internship. Failure to complete the Praxis II requirement will result in failure to complete UCA's MAT Program. I understand that I will receive an "incomplete" (grade of X) in Internship until all requirements have been satisfied.

_____ Date_____
Student

_____ Date_____
Program Coordinator

Appendix D
Professional Development Plan

At this point in your internship program, it is felt you have not shown the teaching or professional behaviors that are at an acceptable level. Our goal in this professional development plan is to help outline areas that need to be addressed as well as to determine appropriate resources to help reach these goals. The following behaviors must be addressed as you continue the program:

1. *Dispositions: Relationships with Others and Communication (See Rubric):*

   - Email communication responded to in a timely manner (within twenty-four hours)
   - Email communication written in professional, courteous language
   - Acceptance of constructive criticism and assistance both from school personnel (math and literacy coaches, assistant principal, etc.) as well as from UCA faculty

2. *TESS Domain 2 (Based on Classroom Observations):*

   - 2a: Creating an environment of respect and rapport: (Shown improvement from 1.0 to 2.0)
     - Observations state students show little respect or rapport for you or their peers. This is noted as a major problem in the classroom.
     - Observation 2 was better, but it was noted after fifteen to twenty minutes, the students were restless and bored.
   - 2b: Establishing a culture for learning: (Shown improvement from 1.5 to 2.0)
     - Observations state students are not taking learning seriously and seemed to show little pride in their work.
   - 2c: Managing classroom procedures: (1.5 — No improvement)

- Observations state materials are not readily accessible and routines are not in place.
- 2d: Managing student behavior: (Shown improvement from 1.0 to 1.5 to 2.0 in March)
    - Observations state the teacher yells. Your reflection states noticing they didn't want to or choose to listen. "They didn't follow rules and were completely disrespectful to me and their peers."
- 2e: Organizing physical safety: (Shown improvement from 1.0 to 1.5 to 2.0 in March)
    - Observations state students are climbing between wires connected to computer. Students were handling computers and Smartboard when they were supposed to be working. Students were running across the room and threw things, and two boys hit each other as they left the classroom and entered the hallway.
- Rules and transitions need to be practiced.

3. *TESS Domain 3 (Based on Classroom Observations):*
    - 3a: Communicating with students: 2.0
        - While you earned a 2, it's concerning that directions and procedures had to be repeated multiple times. To stay as a 2, improvement needs to be shown.
    - 3b: Using questioning and discussion techniques: 2.0
        - While you earned a 2, it's concerning that you had to repeat yourself multiple times because students weren't listening. To stay as a 2, improvement needs to be shown.
    - 3c: Engaging students in learning: (1.5—down from 2.0—back up to 2.0 in March)
        - Observation noted it was difficult to keep students on task.
        - Spending one hour on comma instruction is not developmentally appropriate.
    - 3d: Using assessment in instruction: 2.0 (Down to 1.5 in March)
        - While you earned a 2, it's concerning that the observer noted it was difficult to see students assess or take pride in their work. To stay as a 2, improvement needs to be shown.
        - In the second observation it was noted you used whiteboards for immediate assessment. Great strategy, but it was noted

that closer observation needed to be made as several had incorrect answers.

- 3e: Demonstrating flexibility and responsiveness: (1.5—down from 2.0)
    - Observation noted you tried to have control, but you felt it was beyond your control at times.
    - No adjustments were made in the second lesson after students were restless and bored after fifteen to twenty minutes.

Specific Areas of Concern from University Supervisor:

- Has a solid foundation of content knowledge and skills for first grade
- Classroom management—procedures in place for everything—organizing the classroom

Specific Areas of Concern from Department Faculty:

- 2a: "Student interactions are characterized by conflict, sarcasm, or put-downs."
- 2b: "Teacher conveys a negative attitude toward the content."
- 2c: "Students not working with the teacher and are not productively engaged in learning." No transitions.

Specific Areas of Concern from Program Coordinator:

- Email communication and professionalism
    - Professionalism concern echoed by administration
- Our concerns are echoed by administration with regards to classroom management and instruction. The principal stated she had this same type of meeting in December. She has noted, however, she has witnessed some improvement in classroom management in the last four weeks.
- The school is providing:
    - An excellent mentor
    - Math coach
    - Literacy coach
    - Grade-level chair
    - Assistant principal with strong curriculum background

Suggestions for Improvement:

- Work to get a strong knowledge of students through interest inventories, discussion with previous teachers, and communication with parents. Purposely build respect and rapport. Yelling cannot happen.
- Study and utilize the district curriculum maps: specifically with regards to literacy. Do not feel you have to create your own curriculum. Utilize the school district's literacy department and your school's literacy coach.
- Continued improvement with classroom management: Class DoJo, positive reinforcement, research Fred Jones, Harry Wong, Kagan Strategies
- Pacing of lessons: Use a timer both with yourself and with your students.
- Procedures: Provide explicit instruction on steps for everything (sharpening pencils, going to the restroom, gathering supplies, what to do in free time) and practice this often.
- Have back up activities. Down time can cause multiple issues in a classroom. Maximize your instructional time.

To Document Summative Evaluation Growth:

- Email a detailed schedule outlining times for subject areas by Tuesday, March 10, at 4:30 P.M.
- A department faculty member will perform additional impromptu evaluations as needed.
- Evaluations will be utilized to provide evidence for the final, summative evaluation in which no component can score lower than a 2.

Teaching today is a complex profession that requires commitment toward growing professionally and a dedication toward developing the potential within each child one serves. The program is to help prepare you for these challenges.

I understand a failing grade for internship and removal from the program will occur if *any* of the following circumstances occur:

1. Continued areas of concern, with no improvement, with regards to Dispositions (see attached). This includes being professional at all times and timely response to email communication and setting up meetings.
2. Earning a grade of "C" or lower overall.
3. Earning lower than a "2" in any area in the summative evaluation. (This takes into account all of your observations as well as growth.)

Please note the grading policy per the Internship Handbook:

Final grade for the class will be determined based on the assignments in Blackboard/Chalk and Wire. The following formula will be used:

- Educational Philosophy, Guidance and Behavior Plan, Professional Growth Plan, Mid-Semester Checkpoint, Journals, and Survey Completion Certificates = 20 percent
- Lessons and Observations = 25 percent
- Unit/Impact on Student Learning = 20 percent
- Summative Evaluation = 25 percent
- Engagement/Professionalism (includes final submission and Teacher Candidate Information Form) = 10 percent

IMPORTANT: An intern scoring a "1" on any element of the summative TESS will receive a "D" or an "F" for the final internship grade.

_____ Intern

_____ Chair

_____ University Supervisor

_____ Program Coordinator

Appendix E
Professional Agreement

I, _____, recognize that I have failed thus far to exhibit an acceptable level of professional behavior in my internship at _____. I have exhibited unprofessional behavior in the following ways:

- Commented to students in the hallway, "This is a family school not a make your family school."
- Had a conference with the principal and still displayed a lack of professionalism.
- Commented to a student in class when asked where I got my jacket, "I got it from your momma's house."
- Had a conference with the principal again. This incident resulted in parent complaints regarding my unprofessional behavior.
- Not preparing adequately.
- Not having plans completed according to my mentor teacher's needs.
- Not using planning time efficiently.
- Not displaying adequate maturity required of a professional.

In order to remain in Internship and in the Teacher Education program, I understand I must:

1. Remain professional with my teacher, principal, and all students at all times.
2. Demonstrate resourcefulness and the ability/willingness to effectively prepare and to follow my mentor teacher's modeling of lessons.
3. Adhere to all of my mentor teacher's and supervisor's expectations and deadlines.

I understand the following consequences will occur following *one* complaint from a teacher, parent, or administrator:

1. Upon the next complaint, I will be removed immediately from _____. If an alternative placement can be found, I will be replaced.
2. If an alternative placement cannot be found, I will receive an "X" and will have to reapply for internship in the spring.
3. If the situation requires, I can receive a failing grade in internship and be removed from the program.

I understand that failure to meet the above requirements and all requirements specified in the Internship Handbook may result in my being removed from Internship and possibly from the Teacher Education program.

_____ Student

_____ Chair

_____ University Supervisor

_____ Program Coordinator

_____ Mentor Teacher

About the Authors

Amy Thompson is from Conway, Arkansas. She is married to Daniel Thompson, and together they have one son, Matthew, who is a political science major with a desire to teach and coach in middle or high school currently attending the University of Central Arkansas. Amy's home also consists of five rescue dogs: Gizmo, Shelby, Callie, Maggie, and Hooch.

Amy graduated with a BSE in elementary education from the University of Central Arkansas and then went on to obtain a MSE in reading education from the University of Arkansas at Little Rock. Upon obtaining her teaching license, Amy was hired to teach fourth grade, later moving to third grade, at Fulbright Elementary in the Little Rock School District in Little Rock, Arkansas. There, Amy led many committees at both the school and district level. Amy also led much professional development for the school and district, leading her to finding a passion for working with teachers. In 2005, Amy was the first person at her school to obtain National Board Certification. She did so in literacy and began to serve the state through coordinating workshops and support groups, mentoring teachers throughout the process. She recently renewed her certification.

Currently, Amy works for the University of Central Arkansas as the Master of Arts in Teaching program coordinator and Master of Arts in Teaching field placement coordinator. She also serves as a clinical instructor currently teaching the Reading Difficulties course. Amy has also taught Curriculum Rationale and Integration of Technology in Teaching, and has supervised interns in the field. In her spare time, she enjoys traveling, reading, going to the movies, and pursuing her PhD in interdisciplinary leadership at the University of Central Arkansas.

From the time **Crystal Voegele** was about five, she knew she wanted to be a teacher. Any opportunity she could find to teach, she took it, even asking for a chalkboard for Christmas one year. Teachers gave her their throwaway books, including some teachers' editions. Not only does she love teaching, but she loves students. That being said, she is a mother to five children—three daughters and two sons—ranging in ages from seventeen to twenty-six. Needless to say, kids are important to her—especially their education.

Crystal's teaching career began in Little Rock School District in Little Rock, Arkansas, over eighteen years ago. Finding herself called to work in urban education, Little Rock presented challenges and myriad opportunities to flex her teaching muscles while exploring creative practices. Throughout her experiences in Little Rock, she found herself learning and wishing her teacher education had better prepared her for the adversities she encountered every day. These early beginnings sparked the passion she now has for teacher education—who better to teach future teachers than passionate educators?

Having now served as a field placement coordinator and instructor, she finds herself, once again, learning. From working with driven professors to networking in the schools, she is inspired on an almost daily basis. As a doctoral candidate, pursuing higher education administration naturally comes as the result of seeking to improve teacher education with a focus on teaching marginalized populations, increasing accessibility, and recruiting teachers from all walks of life. As a first-generation college student, teachers played a significant role in her journey, and she hopes to pay their inspiration forward.

Chris Hogan is a life-long learner who is committed to helping improve student learning by preparing teacher candidates to recognize and use their strengths to become effective teachers in the classroom. Best known for using amusing examples of experiences in public education, she teaches diversity and supervises and instructs practicum students and interns during their field experiences.

Chris serves currently as a clinical instructor in the Master of Arts in Teaching program at the University of Central Arkansas in Conway, Arkansas. During her career, she has taught in elementary- and middle-level suburban and urban public schools. She has served as principal at a rural elementary and middle school, and has managed and reported on both federal and state programs in the district.

Chris believes that successful educators achieve success through being creative problem solvers and establishing a network of support. She encourages her students to recognize and explore their strengths and to use them in their classrooms. She helps her students to identify their weaknesses and build a network of resources and support to improve them.

www.ingramcontent.com/pod-product-compliance
Lightning Source LLC
Chambersburg PA
CBHW021801230426
43669CB00006B/153